Contents

Getting started	Page 4
Programming the buttons	Page 10
Making a simple animation	Page 14
Making a more complicated animation	Page 18
Using looping commands	Page 21
Making a light meter	Page 24
Making a night light	Page 28
Making a thermometer	Page 34
Making a step counter	Page 38
Making a compass	Page 42
Making a reaction game	Page 48
Wire following game	Page 56
Connecting a speaker to your Microbit	Page 67
Composing a tune	Page 69
Making a tug of war game	Page 77
Making a circuit with a breadboard	Page 88
Primary colours of light	Page 97
Secondary colours of light	Page 103
Making more colours	Page 106
Making a random light generator	Page 108
Generating colour codes	Page 114
Making a flashing light	Page 119

Activity 1 – Getting started

Hello and welcome to the 'Coding with the BBC Micro:bit'. We hope you are excited about learning to code on your own mini-computer. The projects in this book will get gradually more difficult and by the end of the book you will have coded animations, computer games and even created your own circuits. As well as these written instructions, all activities also have their own video instructions which you can find online at

www.fun-science.org.uk/bigboxofcodingvideos

The Microbit can accept four different 'languages' of coding – JavaScript, Blockly, Touch Develop and Python. We are going to be using Blockly for our coding. The first thing you need to do is to plug your Microbit into the computer using the USB cable. The Microbit looks like this...

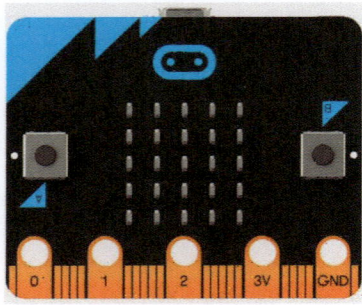

... but it may be a slightly different colour.

The USB cable is a thick black wire with a large flat end and a smaller thin end. It will look something like this.

 CODING

Plug the smaller end of the cable into the Microbit and the larger end of the cable into a USB socket on your computer. Ask a grownup if you aren't sure which is the USB socket. If you visit 'My Computer' or 'This PC' or 'Finder' (On a Mac) you should see MICROBIT on the left-hand side of your screen. This just shows that you have connected your Microbit properly.

Next, you need to open a website browser page. This could be Chrome, Safari, Firefox, Internet Explorer etc. In the address bar, type in makecode.microbit.org and you should see a screen that looks like this.

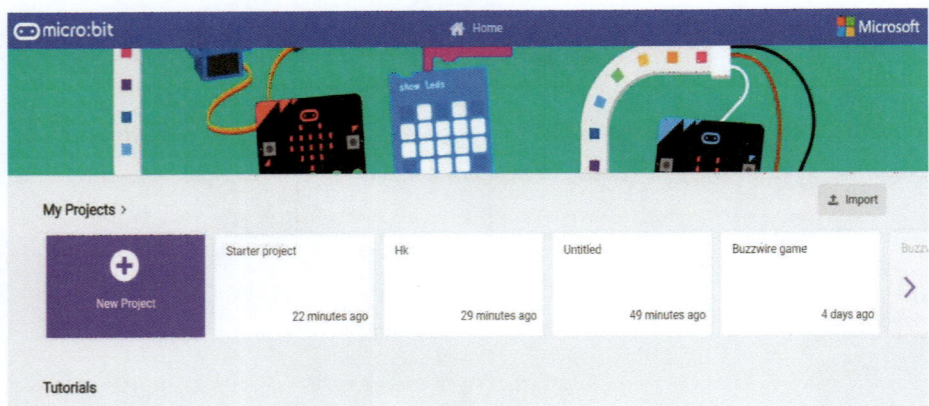

Click on 'New Project' and you will be taken to a screen like this.

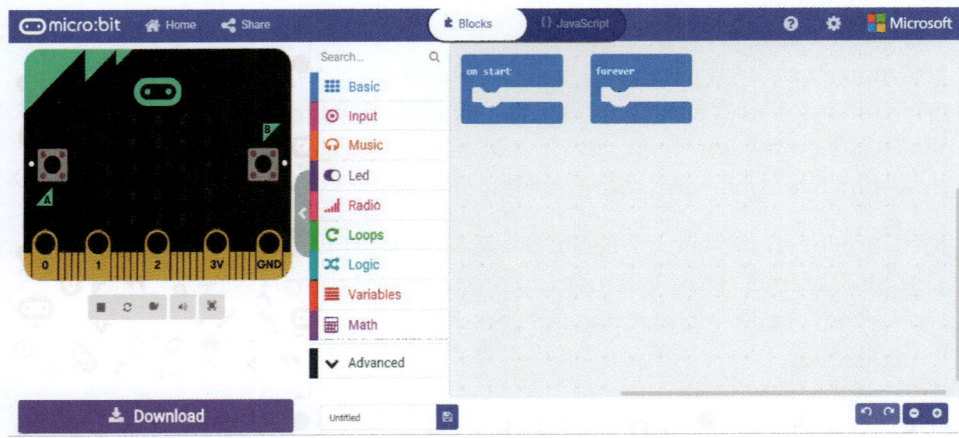

On the left-hand side of the screen you will see a picture that looks exactly like your Microbit! This is a place for you to test out your codes before you download them onto your actual

Microbit. On the right-hand side is where you will be making your code. At the moment, there are two commands on the right-hand side – 'on start' and 'forever'. You can get rid of these by clicking on them and dragging them over to the left. You will then see a bin icon appear and if you let go of the command it will disappear. You can also click on them and press the delete button on your keyboard.

Go ahead and get rid of the 'forever' command and leave the 'on start' command there.

'On start' means what we want the Microbit to do when we turn it on. At the moment, it's not doing anything because there is a gap underneath 'on start'. We need to tell the system to do something by dragging another command into that gap.

Click on basic (blue) and you should see this menu appear:

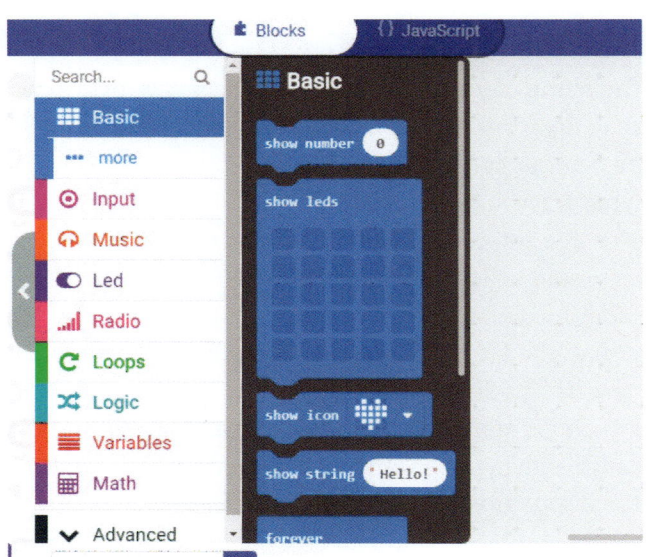

Page | 5

 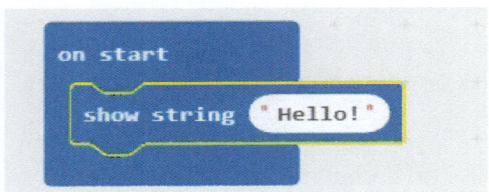

These are all commands that we can ask our Microbit to do when we turn it on. Click and drag 'show string' over to your 'on start' command so that it sits in the gap. Like this:

Now you should see that your Microbit simulator on the left-hand side is saying hello!

You can change the text to whatever you want by double clicking in the box where 'hello' is and typing whatever you want the Microbit to say when you turn it on.

Next, find the box at the bottom which says 'untitled' and replace this with the name of your project. You could call it 'first project' or 'message'. Click the purple 'Download' button and choose somewhere on your computer to save your project. Don't save it directly to your Microbit because the Microbit can only hold one programme at a time so when you next save something onto it your project would be lost. Once you have downloaded your file, you should then go back to 'My Computer' or 'Finder' (or equivalent) and find the file. Click and drag it to the MICROBIT on the left-hand side. An orange light on the Microbit will flash for a few seconds and a window may appear on your screen showing the file moving over. After a few seconds, the light will stop and that means your file is transferred.

If you are having trouble getting started or transferring your programme onto your Microbit, don't forget that you can watch our videos at

www.fun-science.org.uk/bigboxofcodingvideos

Once you have copied your programme onto your Microbit, you will need to unplug it from the USB cable. This means your Microbit has no power! Instead, you need to plug the batteries into the Microbit. Attach your battery pack to the Microbit. It may look something like this.

Insert your batteries into the holder, making sure you get them the correct way around (ask a grownup for help if you aren't sure) and then push the white end of the wire into the square white hole on your Microbit. Your Microbit should turn on and

you should see your message on the screen. That's it, you've completed your first project!

Activity 2 – Programming the buttons

Another thing that you can do, is to programme the Microbit to do different things when you press the A and B buttons. Plug your Microbit into the computer and go back to

Makecode.microbit.org

Open up the project from activity 1.

Click input (purple) and then drag the 'on button A pressed' command to anywhere in your editor. It can be here...

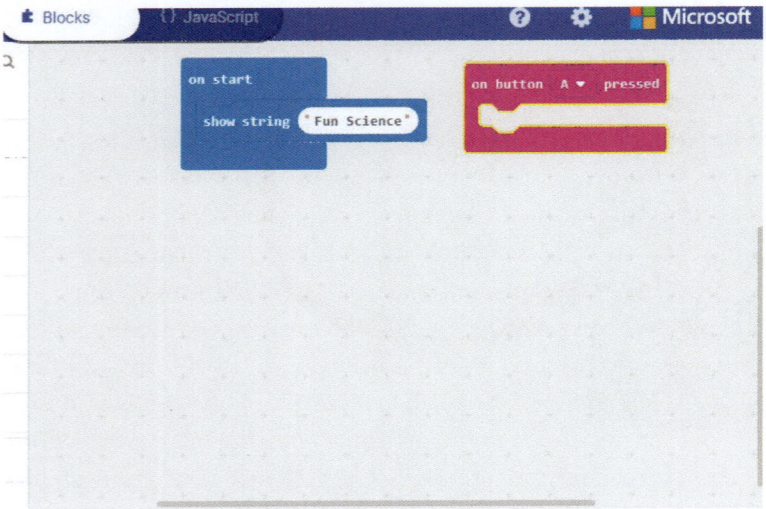

Here…

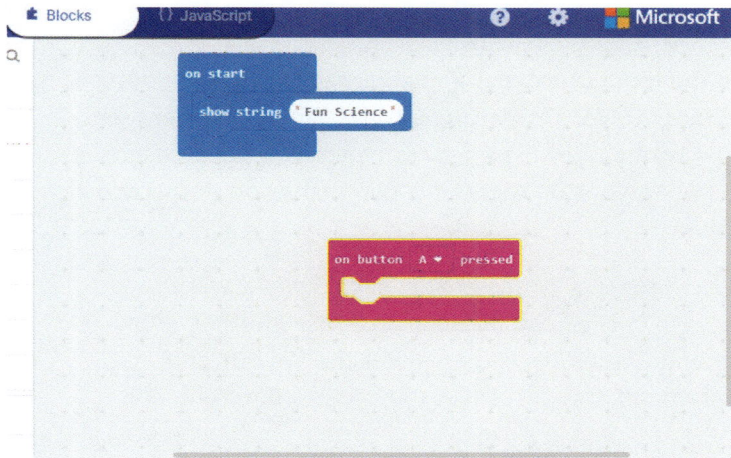

Or anywhere else that you want to put it!

Now, we need to tell the system what we want it to do when we press button A. Just like before, go to the basic (blue) menu and this time, drag the show icon command into the gap under the 'on button A pressed' command. Like this:

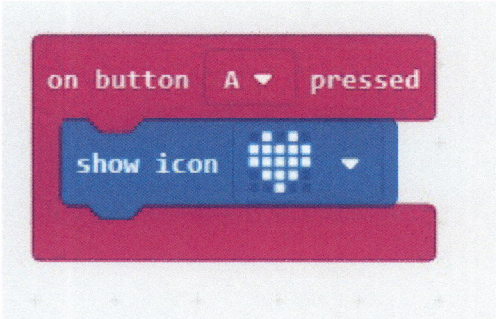

Page | 9

The default icon is a heart and this will be shown by the little lights on your Microbit's screen. You can change this icon by clicking the little white arrow next to the heart and choosing a different picture.

Next, let's programme button B.

Go back to the Input (purple) menu and drag another 'on button A pressed' block to your editor. Again, you can put it wherever you like. The command will be grey to begin with because you can't have two 'on button A pressed' commands on the screen at the same time.

Use the button next to 'A' and change it to B and it will go purple. Go back to the basic menu and choose another 'show icon' command. Drag it to the gap under the 'on button B pressed' command. Use the arrow to choose a different icon.

It should look something like this.

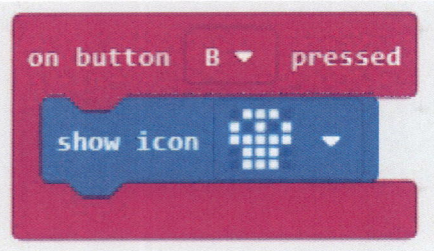

The whole thing should look a bit like this but your commands may be in different places and your text and pictures will be different.

Page | 10

Just like last time click the purple 'Download' button and choose somewhere on your computer to save your project. Remember not to save it directly to your Microbit. Transfer your project to your Microbit, make sure the battery pack is connected, and press the different buttons to see your different pictures.

Activity 3 – Making a simple animation

Now that you know the basics, you are going to be programming your Microbit to show an animation. There are two ways that you can do this and we are going to try both!

The first way is just to set one picture to show when you press button A and another to show when you press button B. You can then quickly press one button then the other to show a flick-book style animation.

Let's give it a go! First open your browser and go to makecode.microbit.org then click on new project.

Remove the 'on start' and 'forever' commands and go to the input (purple) menu and drag the 'on button A pressed' command over to the editor. This time, instead of putting a pre-made icon in the gap, we are going to be making our own!

Go to the basic (blue) menu and drag the 'show leds' command over to the gap under your 'on button A pressed' command. LED stands for Light Emitting Diode. These are the 25 little lights on the front of your Microbit. You should see a grid that looks like this.

Each square in this command block represents an LED on your Microbit. You can click in the squares to draw a picture. Try drawing a smiley face like this.

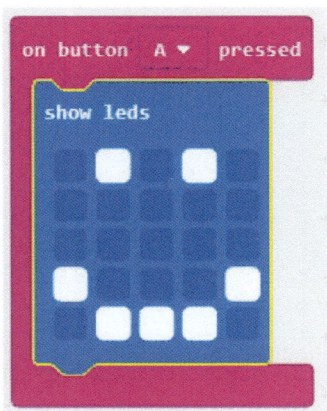

Try using the simulator. When you press button A on the simulator, you should see your smiley face.

Now, let's programme button B.

Just like in the last activity, drag another 'on button A pressed' command over to your screen and use the arrow to change the letter A to B.

Just like before, drag another 'show leds' command to the gap underneath 'on button B pressed'. It should look like this.

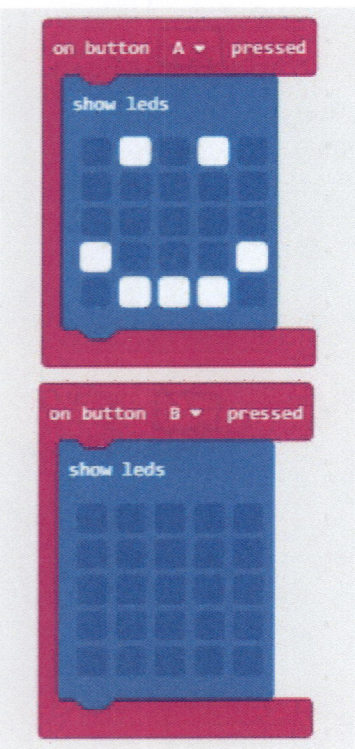

Page | 14

Next, draw a sad face like this

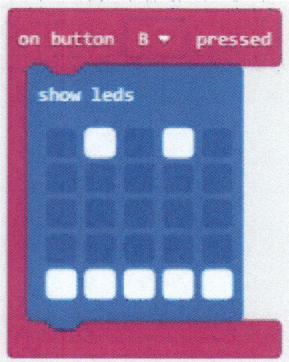

That's it! You are ready to download your project. Give the project a name and download it to your computer then transfer it to your Microbit like we did in the last two activities.

Now, try pressing A then B then A then B on your Microbit and keep doing this really fast. This is like a flick book! It should look like your face is going happy and sad. Can you think of another simple animation with two pictures? Make sure the two pictures are not too different to each other or else it won't look as good.

When you have tried a few different pictures, have a go at the next activity which is a slightly more complicated way of making a longer animation.

Activity 4 - Making a more complicated animation

Let's try and make a more complicated animation with lots of different frames. Frames are the words animators use for each individual picture that is put together to make an animation.

Start a new project and get rid of the 'on start' command but keep the 'forever' command.

Underneath the 'forever' command, drag a 'show leds' command (from the basic menu) and draw the pattern below.

Now, drag another 'show leds' command underneath that first one and draw this pattern on it.

Add another 'show leds' command under that and draw this pattern.

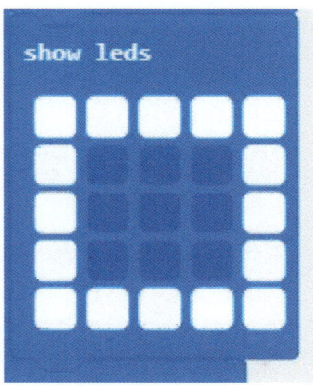

Just one last command to do – put in another 'show leds' command underneath and draw this pattern again.

The whole thing should look like this

Page | 18

Because the commands are all within a 'forever' command, this will keep repeating forever whenever your Microbit is switched on. Can you see your animation running in the simulator on the left hand side? Give your project a name, download it and put it onto your Microbit. Can you see the animation on the Microbit? Try out some different patterns and make your own animation. It can be as long as you like!

Activity 5 – Using looping commands

Let's try one last animation. This time, instead of the animation running all the time, we will set it to only run when the A key is held down using a looping block from the green menu. As soon as you let go of the A button, the animation will stop.

Start a new project and get rid of the 'on start' command.

Go to the loops (green) menu and drag a 'while true do' command under your 'forever' command. It should look like this

Go to the Input (purple) menu and drag a 'button A is pressed' command to replace the blue 'true'. Like this.

Page | 19

This is telling the system that we only want it to play the animation when button A is pressed down. When you release button A it will stop the animation. Now, stack up 'show leds' commands inside this green command block to make an animation, just like before. You could make your own animation up or copy the one below.

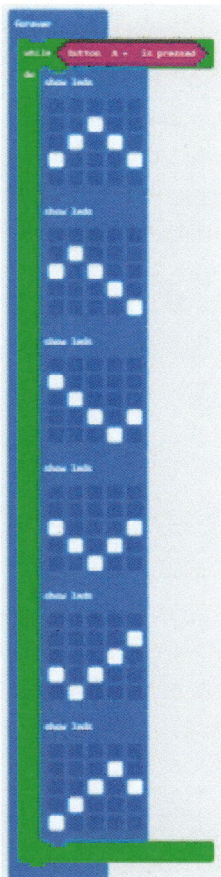

Give your project a name and download it onto your Microbit. Does it work? Keep changing your animation until you are happy with it.

Activity 6 – Making a light meter

In this activity, we are going to be using the light sensor that is built into your Microbit. In fact, the LEDS on your Microbit actually work as light sensors as well as lights! The way this works is the 6 LEDs circled below all take a light reading and then the system works out an average of these numbers to calculate how much light is around in the room. In simple terms it can tell you how light or dark your room is.

Light sensors are used in lots of computers and electronic devices that need to either turn on when it's dark or turn off when it's dark. One use is in a night light that turns on when it's dark and off when it's light. Most mobile phones have light sensors so that the screen can get brighter when there is lots of light around and dimmer when the room is darker.

Start off by going to makecode.microbit.org and starting a new project. You can delete the 'on start' and 'forever' blocks.

First, we need to create a variable and define it. A variable is something that can change (like light level, temperature, speed etc.) and defining it just means telling the system what it means.

Go to the red variables menu and click 'make a variable'. Call the variable 'level'. You should then see these options appear.

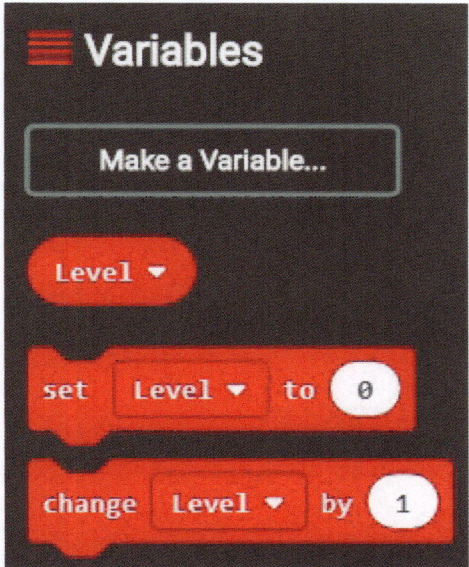

Drag the 'set level to 0' block onto your screen. It will show as grey for the moment because you haven't put it underneath a basic or input command. That's ok, we will sort that out later.

We have now set the variable but next we need to define it. At the moment, the system doesn't know what the word 'level' means so we have to tell it. Go to the purple input menu and find the 'light level' command. Drag this to replace the 0 in 'set level to 0'. It should look like this.

Page | 23

Next, we need to tell the system when we want this to happen. Let's use the 'on button A pressed' command. Can you remember where this one is?

It's in the purple menu! Click and drag an 'on button A pressed' command over to your screen and then put the 'set level to light level' block that you created earlier underneath it. Like this.

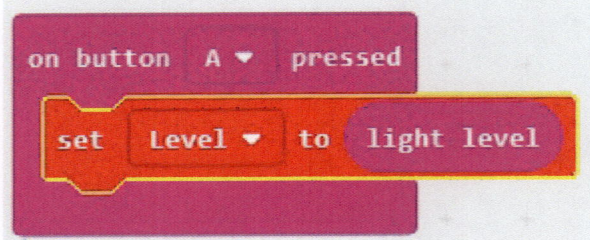

Now we have told the system that when we press button A, 'level' means 'light level'. Next, we need to tell it to show us what that light level is on the screen.

Go to the basic (blue) menu and drag a 'show number' command under the 'set level to light level' command.

Page | 24

Lastly, we just need to replace the 0 with 'level' to tell the system that we want to see the level of light displayed on the screen.

Go to the red variables menu and drag a 'level' command to replace the number 0.

The final programme should look like this

Download your programme onto your Microbit and see what happens when you press the A button. A reading of 0 means pitch black and a reading of 255 means really bright! Try and find the darkest room in your house and the brightest room or try shining a torch on the Microbit and moving the torch closer and further away from the LEDs.

Activity 7 – Making a night light

Now you've had a play with the light sensor reading, let's make a night light that automatically comes on in the dark and goes off in the light.

Come back to the Blockly editor (makecode.microbit.org) and start a new project. Call this project something like 'night light'. We are going to be using the 'forever' command and you can remove the 'on start' command.

In this activity, we are going to be telling the system that if the light level drops below a certain level, we would like it to turn the lights on the Microbit on.

To do this, we need one of the logic blocks from the light blue/green menu. The command we are using is the one that looks a bit like a giant E and has 'if true then _____ else_____' written on it. Drag it onto your screen underneath the forever command.

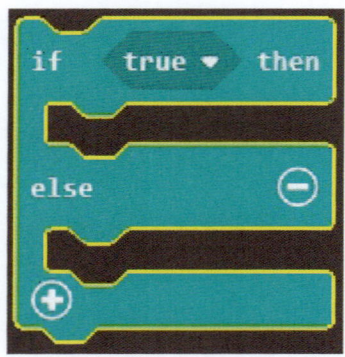

This command basically tells the system that if something is true then it needs to do an action but if something is not true then it

needs to do something else. What we need to tell it next is what the 'something' is and also what the two different actions we want it to take are.

First, we need to replace the true block with something else. Go back to the logic menu and find this block

Drag it so that it replaces the 'true' diamond like this.

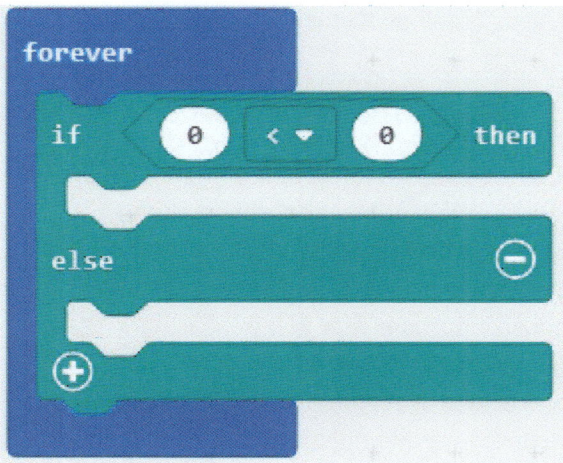

At the moment this doesn't make much sense because the sign < means 'less than' so this command says 'if 0 is less than 0' which is impossible! We need to replace the first 0 with 'light level' from the purple menu. It will look like this.

Page | 27

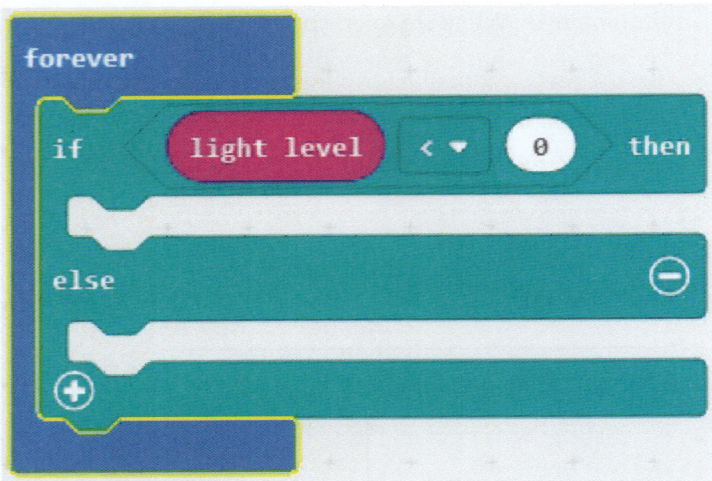

This still doesn't make any sense because the light level can't be less than 0 as that's the lowest possible number and means pitch black! We need to change this 0 to a different number. When you were testing the light sensor earlier you will have got a bit of an idea of which number means quite dark, which number means quite light etc. Choose a number that you think is dark enough for your night light to turn on. Don't make it too low because it's rare that your bedroom will have absolutely no light, even in the dark, because of the moon and streetlights. I'm going to go for 100.

Next, we need to tell the system what we want it to do when the light level is less than 100. We are making a night light so we want it to light up. Go to the basic (blue) menu and drag a 'show leds' command to below the 'if light level < 0 then' command. You can then click on the LEDs that you would like to be turned on. I've decided to turn them all on but you may want to make a pattern.

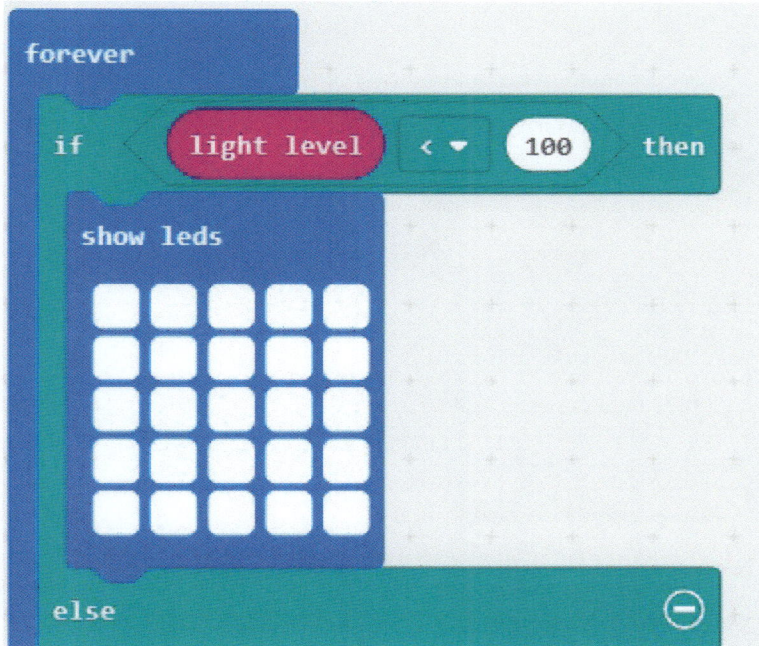

Next, we need to decide how bright we want our night light to be. This probably depends on what you want your light to be used for. If it's a night light for beside your bed you may want it to be quite dim so it doesn't keep you awake. If you want your light to be used as an emergency light that will turn on if all the power goes out in your house, you would probably want it to be really bright!

Go to the purple Led menu and click on more. Select the 'set brightness' command and drag it to above your 'show leds' command. Just like with the light sensor, 255 means very bright and 0 means completely off. Choose how bright you would like your LEDs to be. I've chosen 255 because I want my night light to be very bright!

The last thing we need to do is to tell the system to turn all the lights off if the light level is not below 100. We are going to go to the blue basic menu and drag a 'clear screen' command to underneath the word 'else' like this.

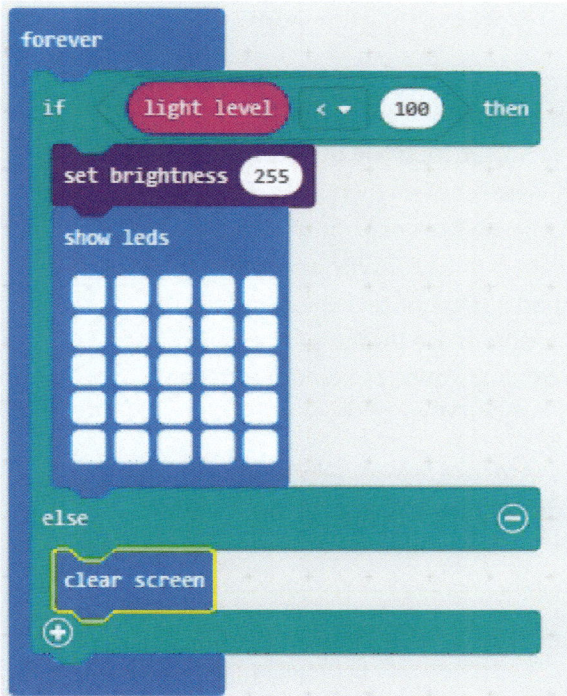

This tells the system that if the light level is less than 100 we would like it to show all the LEDs very brightly but if it is higher than 100 we would like it to clear the screen/not show any LEDs.

Download the project onto your Microbit and test it out. If it lights up too often, change the 'if light level < 100' to be a lower number so it only lights up when it is really dark. If your night light is too bright, change the 'set brightness 255' to a lower number to make a dimmer light. If the programme isn't working, make sure your Microbit is placed face up on a flat surface. If you have a room in your house with no windows, go to that room and turn the lights in the room on. Now turn the lights off!

Activity 8 - Making a thermometer

Your Microbit also has a built-in temperature sensor. This detects how hot the CPU (central processing unit) in your Microbit is. It tends to be a few degrees hotter than the outside world because the Microbit generates a little bit of its own heat. Remember, you should not use your Microbit in very hot or very cold temperatures as it could get damaged. With the light sensor we tested it by shining lights on it. Do not test the temperature sensor by putting the Microbit in the 'fridge or the oven! Just take it to different parts of your house to see the different temperatures inside and outside the house.

To make a temperature sensor we are actually going to do almost exactly what we did when we made our light meter reader. Start off by going to makecode.microbit.org and starting a new project. You can delete the 'on start' and 'forever' blocks.

Just like before, we need to create a variable and define it.

Go to the red variables menu and click 'make a variable'. Call the variable 'level' just like we did before. You should then see these options appear.

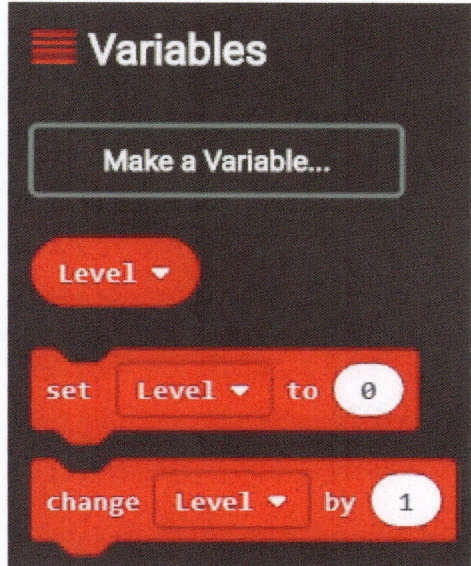

Drag the 'set level to 0' block onto your screen. It will show as grey for the moment because you haven't put it underneath a basic or input command.

We have now set the variable but next we need to define it like we did last time. Go to the purple input menu and find the 'temperature' command. Drag this to replace the 0 in 'set level to 0'. It should look like this.

Next, we need to tell the system when we want this to happen. Let's use the 'on button B pressed' command this time. It's in the purple menu! Click and drag an 'on button A pressed' command

over to your screen, change the A to a B and then put the 'set level to temperature' block that you created earlier underneath it. Like this.

So now, we have told the system that when we press button B, 'level' means temperature in degrees Celsius. Next, we need to tell it to show us what that temperature is on the screen.

Go to the basic (blue) menu and drag a 'show number' command under the 'set level to temperature' command.

Lastly, we just need to replace the 0 with 'level' to tell the system that we want to see the temperature displayed on the screen.

Go to the red variables menu and drag a 'level' command to replace the number 0.

The final programme should look like this

You can now download this onto your Microbit and when you press B you should see the temperature in degrees Celcius. If you have a thermometer in your house, compare the two together to see how accurate the Microbit is. Remember it's likely to be a bit hotter than your thermometer says it is because the Microbit makes a bit of heat.

To run the light sensor and temperature sensor in the same programme, you just need to put the programme from the light sensor onto the screen at the same time as the programme from the temperature sensor. It will look like this.

Now, when you press button A you should see the light level and when you press button B you will see the temperature.
Download the programme and give it a go! Remember not to put your Microbit in the oven!

Activity 9 – Making a step counter

Inside your Microbit is something called an 'accelerometer' which can detect movement so it can tell you if your Microbit is shaken, turned or dropped. Most phones and tablets have accelerometers in them so that they can turn the screen when you turn the phone. We are going to be using that accelerometer to turn your Microbit into a step-counter which will be able to tell you how many steps you have taken.

Start a new project and get rid of the 'on start' block.

The first thing we need to do is define a variable like we did in the light sensor and thermometer projects. Click the red variables menu and click make a variable. Name your variable 'steps'. Drag the 'change steps by 1' onto your screen. It will be grey but that is ok!

We are going to design this so that you will hold the Microbit in your hand when you run. When you run, you tend to shake your arms up and down. On one step you will move your right arm up and then on the next step you will move it down. This up and down movement is one 'shake'. For every two steps you take, each arm does one shake. So, we need to tell the Microbit to move the number of steps up by two every time you shake it. Change the number from 1 to 2 and then grab an 'on shake' command from the purple input menu and put it on your screen. Put the two commands together like this.

Now, we need to tell the system to show us (in lights) how many steps we have taken in total.

Inside the 'forever' command, you should put a 'show number' command from the blue basic menu. Change the number 0 to 'steps' from the variables menu. It will look like this.

So now, the system knows to keep showing you the number of steps you have done and to keep increasing that number by two every time you shake the Microbit.

The last thing we need to make is a reset button to put the number of steps back to 0.

Drag an 'on button A pressed' command from the purple input menu onto your screen. Change A to A + B using the drop-down menu. Like this

Page | 37

CODING

[on button A+B pressed block]

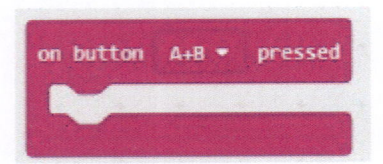

Lots of devices ask you to press two buttons to reset them instead of just one. This is because you are less likely to do this by accident.

Now we need to tell the system what we would like it to do when we press the A and B buttons at the same time.

Go to the red variables menu and drag a 'set steps to 0' command into the right place like this.

[on button A+B pressed with set Steps to 0]

That's our step counter finished but there is one optional extra we can add on.

Sometimes, when we have done lots of steps, the system will be trying to show us one number and then we shake the Microbit again and we want it to stop the first number and show us the next one immediately.

Imagine that we had done 1000 steps and the system is scrolling the number 1000 across the screen. This takes around 5 seconds. Whilst this is happening, we take another step. We don't want to have to wait for the number 1000 to go across the screen before the system shows us 1002 because that 1000 is not relevant anymore. Anytime we have to wait for a system to finish one

Page | 38

thing before it does the thing we actually want it to do, we call this 'lag'.

To get rid of this lag we need to tell the system that every time it is shaken it can stop whatever number it was trying to tell us and move straight onto the next one.

Go to the purple Led menu and click more. Drag a 'stop animation' command underneath your 'change steps by 2' command. The whole thing should look like this.

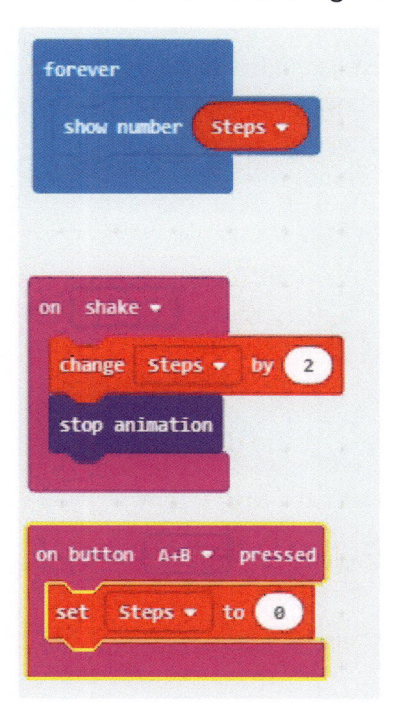

Download this to your Microbit and hold the Microbit and power pack in one hand. Go for a run and make sure you swing your arms!

Activity 10 – Making a compass

Did you know, the Earth is one big giant magnet? Your Microbit has a built-in magnetic field sensor which means it can work out whether it is pointing North, South, East or West. We are going to build a programme to turn your Microbit into a compass.

Start a new project and call it something like 'compass'

Remove the 'on start' command but keep the 'forever' command.

Next, we need to create a new variable just like in the step counter activity. Go to the red variables menu, click 'Make a Variable' and call it degrees. Drag the 'set degrees to 0' command to underneath the forever command. Like this.

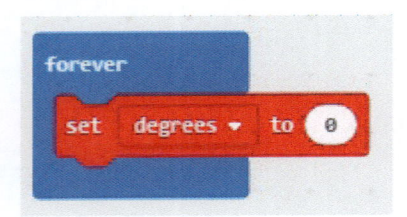

Next, we need to define the variable. Degrees is going to mean whereabouts on the compass we are. So, let's tell the system.

Go to the purple input menu and drag 'compass heading' to replace the 0 like this.

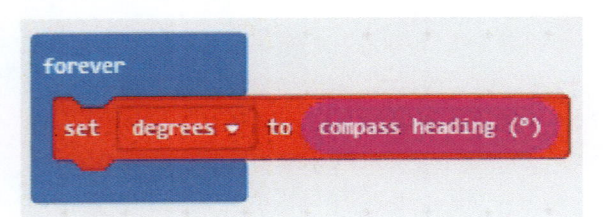

CODING

But what does this actually mean? A compass is basically a big circle and 'degrees' is how far around that circle we are. Look at the picture below. Can you see all the numbers around the outside? We call these degrees. So North is from around 316 degrees to 45 degrees. East is from 46 degrees to 135 degrees; South is from 136 degrees to 225 degrees and West is from 226 degrees to 315 degrees.

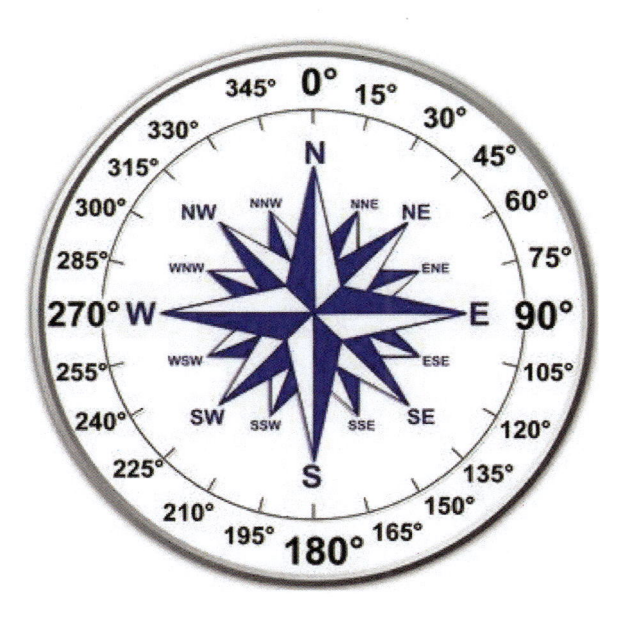

The magnetic field detector in the Microbit will work out how many degrees around that circle we are and then we are going to programme it to tell us if we are at North, East, South or West using the LEDs.

Go to the light blue logic menu and drag a an 'if true then _____ else_____' command under your 'set degrees to compass heading' command. Like this.

This is like what we did when we made our night light. Next, we need to replace that 'true' command with a 0 < 0 command exactly like when we made our night light. Grab the command from the light blue logic menu and drag it to replace the 'true' block. Like this.

CODING

Remember, this doesn't really make sense because it is saying if 0 is less than 0 and 0 can't be less than 0! So, we need to tell the system that if 'degrees' is less than 45, we are facing North and so the screen should show the letter N.

Replace the first 0 with 'degrees' from the red variables menu and replace the second 0 with the number 45. Like this.

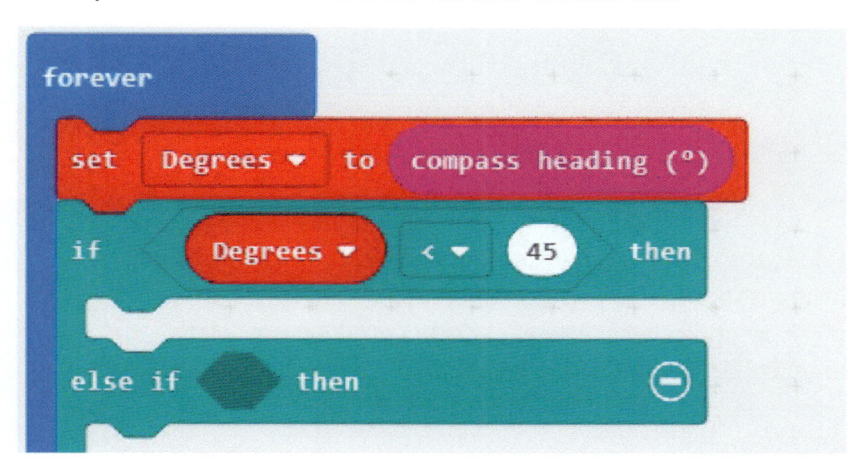

```
forever
    set Degrees ▼ to  compass heading (°)
    if  Degrees ▼  < ▼  45  then

    else if          then
```

Next, go to the blue basic menu and drag a 'show string' command into the gap underneath 'if degrees < 45' to tell the system what it should show if the degrees are less than 45. Change the string to the letter N. Like this.

Page | 43

So now, the system knows that if the degrees is between 0 and 45 then it should show a letter N on the screen so we know that we are pointing North. This isn't quite right because North should be between 316 degrees and 360 degrees as well as 0 and 45 degrees. But it's half way there! We will worry about that extra bit later.

Next, let's do the same for East, South and West. You will need to click the little '+' sign underneath the word 'else' three times to get three extra gaps like this.

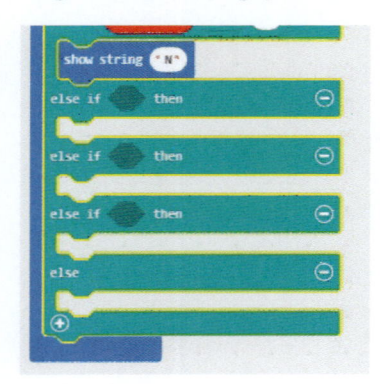

Page | 44

CODING

Next, fill these in exactly like we did for North but for the other directions. You may want to copy the picture below to help you.

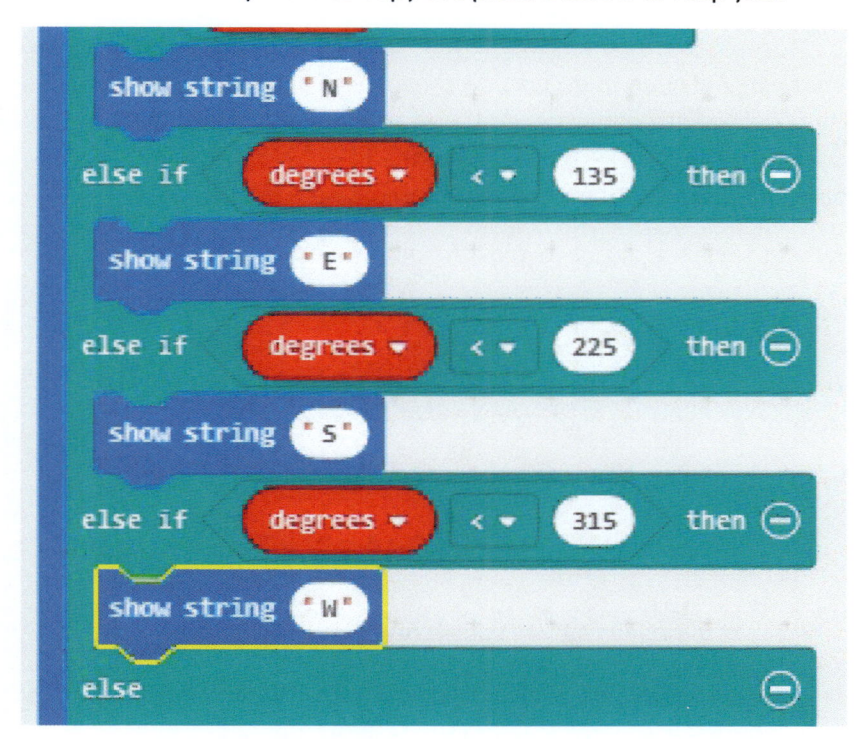

```
show string " N "
else if  degrees ▼  < ▼  135   then ⊖
    show string " E "
else if  degrees ▼  < ▼  225   then ⊖
    show string " S "
else if  degrees ▼  < ▼  315   then ⊖
    show string " W "
else                                ⊖
```

Finally, we just need to fill in that bottom gap with 'show string N'. This is telling the system that if degrees is more than 315 it should show the letter N because that will mean it is pointing North. Remember that's the bit we missed out earlier.

Now, you just need to download your project onto your Microbit and give it a try. When you turn on your Microbit for the first time, something strange will happen. You may see some words scroll across the screen or lots of dots filling the screen. This is because every time you put a new programme that uses the compass onto your Microbit, the system needs to calibrate itself. In this case, the word calibrate means it needs to work out where it is!

What you will need to do is to tilt the screen in the direction of any LEDs that are not lit up until they all light up. Then your compass will be ready to use. If you need any help with this, there is a video about calibrating your compass at

www.fun-science.org.uk/bigboxofcodingvideos

Test your compass out. Like a normal compass, the compass on your Microbit can go wrong if you put it near a magnet or some metal because it will then pick up the magnet instead of the Earth.

If you like, you could put in even more commands to be able to show North East, North West, South East and South West.

Activity 11 - Making a reaction game

This next game will test your reactions. You will be creating a game where a light moves across the screen from left to right and you have to press the A button when it is in the middle of the screen. If you press the button at the right time, you get a point. If you press it when the light is not in the middle, you lose the game.

The first thing we need to do is create a variable and name it 'sprite'. In coding, a sprite is a moveable item that can either move on its own or be controlled by the player. 'Steve' in Minecraft is a sprite. Our sprite is going to be a single light that moves across the screen.

CODING

Click in the variables menu, click 'make a variable' and name your variable sprite. Drag the 'set sprite to 0' command to the 'on start' block.

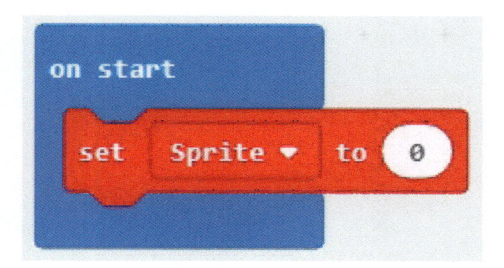

Next, we are going to be using the dark green 'game' menu. You can find this under 'advanced' on the left-hand side. Find the 'create sprite at x 2 y 2' command and drag it to replace the 0 in 'set sprite to 0' like this.

So what does this mean? Each of the lights on your Microbit has its own unique number made up of an 'x' value and a 'y' value. We call these co-ordinates. Look at the grid on the next page. The light circled is 3,2. Can you see why? Its x value (the numbers along the top) is 3 and its y value (the numbers along the side) is 2. Can you work out the value of the very centre light?

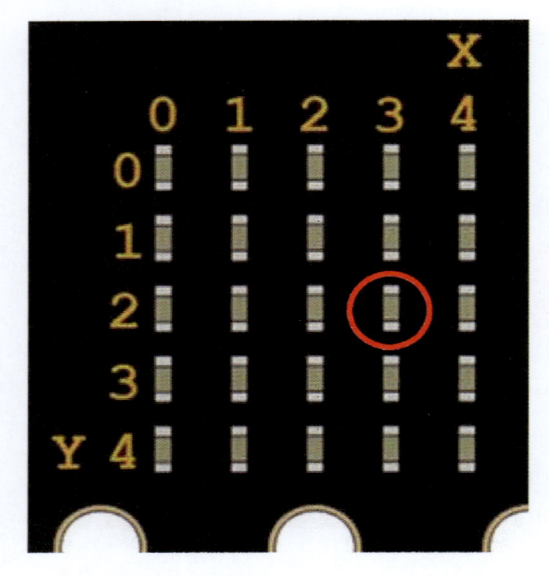

It's 2,2 because the x value is 2 and the y value is 2.

So, when we created this command…

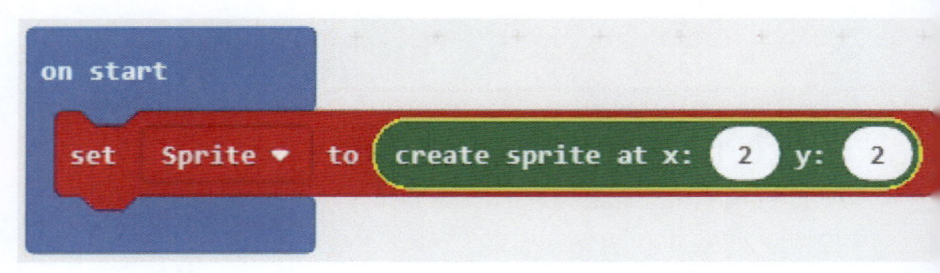

…we told the system to create a 'sprite' (a light) right in the centre of the screen (at 2,2). You should see it in the simulator on the left-hand side.

Now, we want to make the sprite move from side to side across the screen. Go back to the 'game' menu and find the 'sprite

Page | 48

move by 1' command and drag it into the 'forever' command block. Like this.

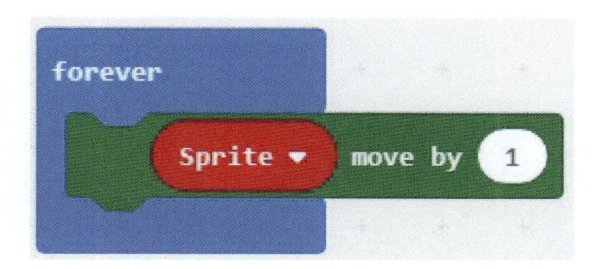

```
forever
    Sprite ▼  move by  1
```

This will make the little light start moving to the right. At the moment, the light moves to the right but then it stops once it gets to the side of the screen. We want it to bounce back and keep moving.

Go back to the game menu and find the command 'sprite, if on edge bounce'. Put this underneath 'sprite move by 1'.

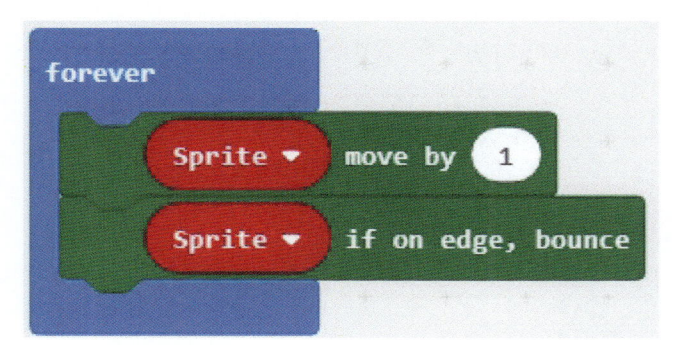

```
forever
    Sprite ▼  move by  1
    Sprite ▼  if on edge, bounce
```

Now, when the light reaches the edge of the screen, it will bounce back in the other direction. This will keep going forever because it's in the forever command!

At the moment, it's quite fast so let's slow it down. Go to the basic menu and grab a 'pause' command and put it under the 'sprite if on edge, bounce' command. Like this. The bigger the number, the slower the sprite will move and the easier the game will be.

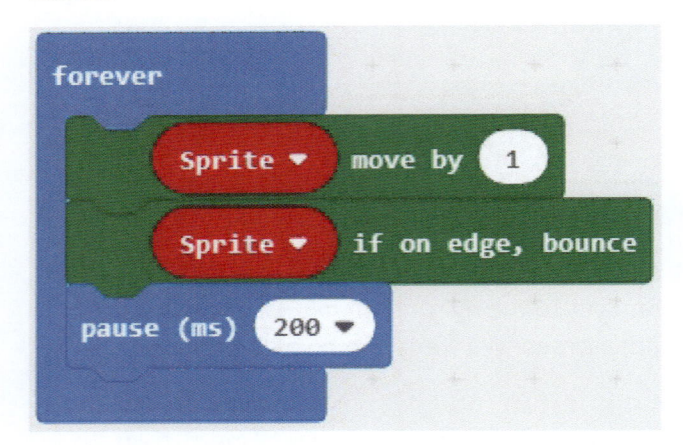

The last thing we need to do is to tell the system what happens when button A is pressed and when the game is won or lost. Get an 'on button A pressed' command from the purple input menu and put it on your screen. Go to the logic menu and get an 'if true then _____ else_____' command and put it inside the 'on button A pressed' command. Like this.

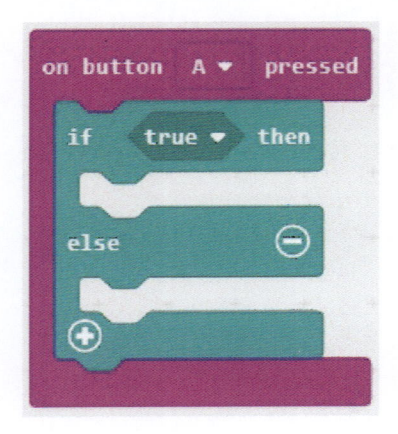

We need to tell the system that if we press the A button when the sprite is at 2,2 (in the middle) we get a point but if we press it at any other time, we lose the game. Go to the logic menu and get a 'if 0 = 0' command to replace the 'true' command.

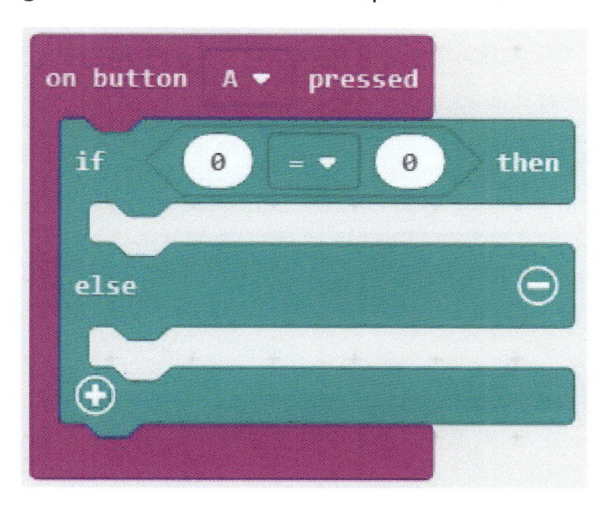

Go to the game menu and replace the first 0 with 'sprite x' and the second 0 with a number 2 like this.

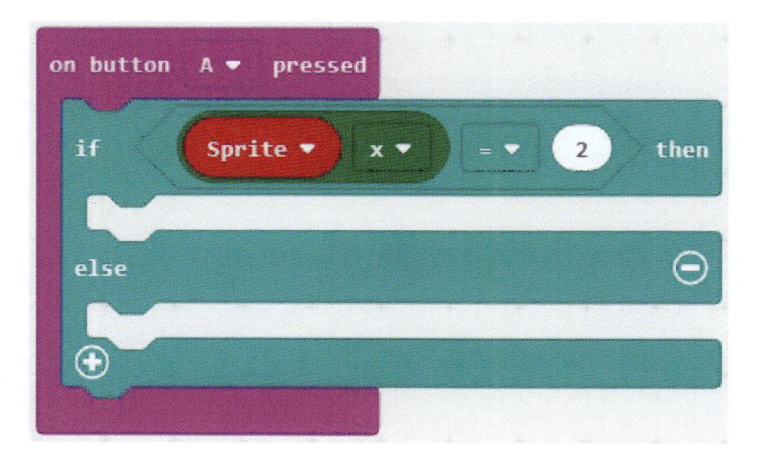

This tells the system that it needs to do something if the sprite's x (horizontal) position is 2 and something else if it is anything else (0, 1, 3 or 4).

We don't need to worry about the y position because the sprite doesn't move up and down so its y position is always 2.

Now, we just need to tell it what the two options are.

If the sprite's x position is 2, the light is in the middle, so we want the system to increase the score by 1. Go to the game menu, find the 'change score by 1' command and drag it under the 'if sprite x = 2' command.

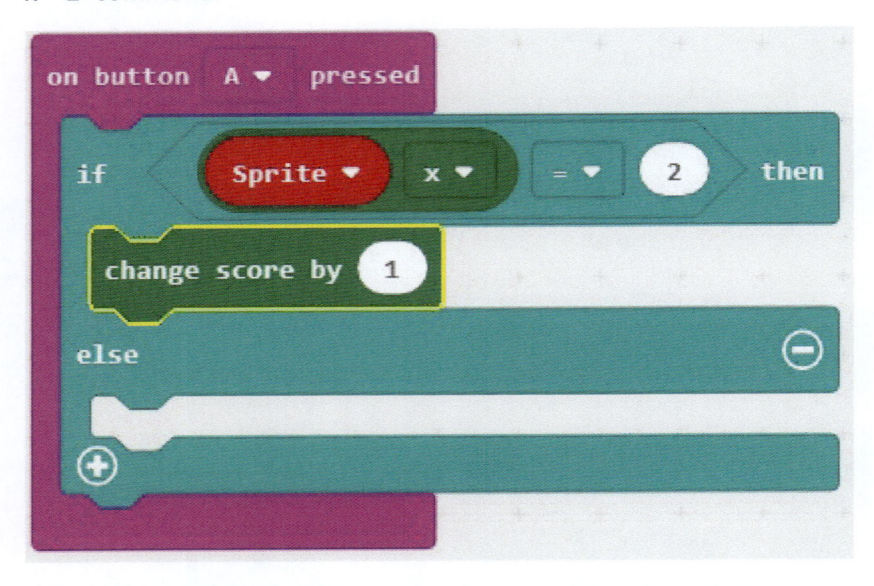

```
on button A pressed
    if Sprite x = 2 then
        change score by 1
    else

```

If we press the button when the sprite isn't in the middle (when x does not equal 2) then we have lost the game. To tell the system this, go to the game menu and drag a 'game over' command under 'else'. The system has a built-in game over sequence which

Page | 52

plays a little animation, scrolls the words game over and then shows you your score. The final code will look like this.

```
on start
    set Sprite ▼ to create sprite at x: 2 y: 2

forever
    Sprite ▼ move by 1
    Sprite ▼ if on edge, bounce
    pause (ms) 200 ▼

on button A ▼ pressed
    if  Sprite ▼ x ▼ = ▼ 2  then
        change score by 1
    else
        game over
```

Download this and give it a go! After you have lost the game you will need to press A and B together to restart it. If it is too easy, increase the speed by putting a smaller number in the pause command. If it's too difficult, decrease the speed by putting a bigger number in the pause command.

Page | 53

Activity 12 - Wire following game

In this activity, you are going to create a wire following game. It's like a buzz wire game – without the buzz! The actual coding for this project is fairly simple, but you will also need to have two alligator test leads, a short piece of conductive (e.g. copper) wire and blue tack to build a game which will connect to your Micro:bit. You can buy copper wire in most craft stores. You will create a maze out of conductive wire and a separate hook, also out of conductive wire. The aim of the game is to pass the hook around the maze without it touching the maze. If it touches the maze, you get one 'loss'. The aim of the game is to pass the hook around the maze with the least possible number of losses.

In this project, we need to set up a scoring system to count your 'losses' and tell our Micro:bit when to display the amount of 'losses' We also need to set up a system to be able to reset the game once you have played it.

Start by visiting makecode.microbit.org and clicking on 'new project'. You can name your new project something like 'buzz wire' or 'wire following game'.

You can delete the 'forever' and 'on start' commands because we don't need them for this project. You may decide later to put them back in so that your Micro:bit shows a welcome message or a picture when you turn it on.

The first step is to tell your system that a new game will start when the player presses button A. Click 'Input' (purple) and then drag an 'on button A pressed' command onto your screen.

CODING

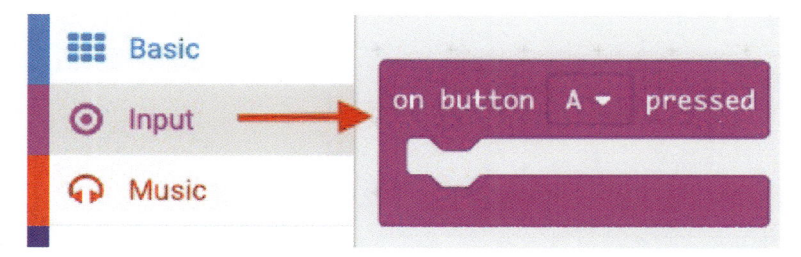

At the beginning of the game, we need the number of 'losses' to be 0 but before we can do that, we need to create a 'losses' variable. This number will be the number of times that your hook has touched your maze. Click on 'Variables' (red) and then 'Make a new Variable'. Name the variable losses.

Drag the 'set losses to 0' command to your 'on button A pressed' command.

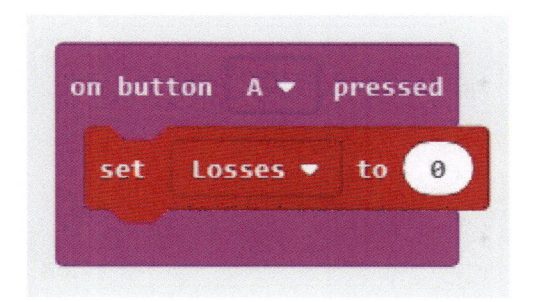

This will reset the number of losses to 0 when you press the A button.

Next, we need to tell the system to display the number of losses (0) when the A button is pressed so that you know it's been reset. To do this, first drag a 'show number' command from 'Basic' (blue) to underneath your 'set losses to 0' command.

Page | 55

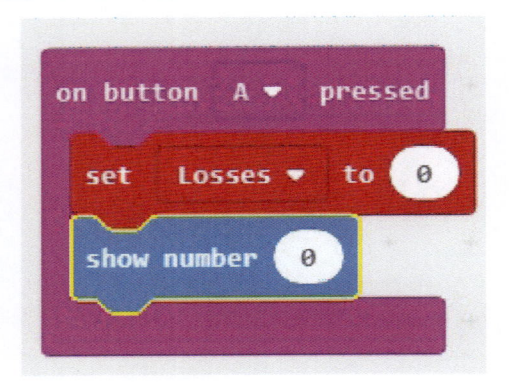

Then click on Variables (red) and drag the **Losses ▼** button into the place of the 0 so that your screen looks like the picture below.

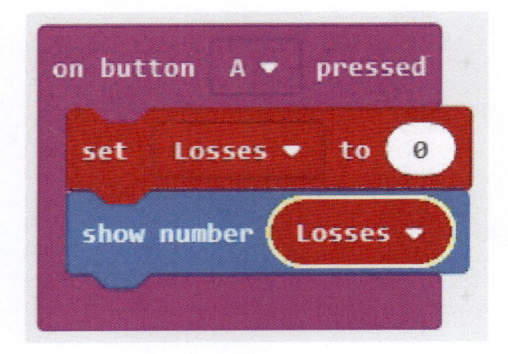

CODING

Test your script using the tester on the left of the screen. Clicking button A should display the number of losses, which has been set to 0.

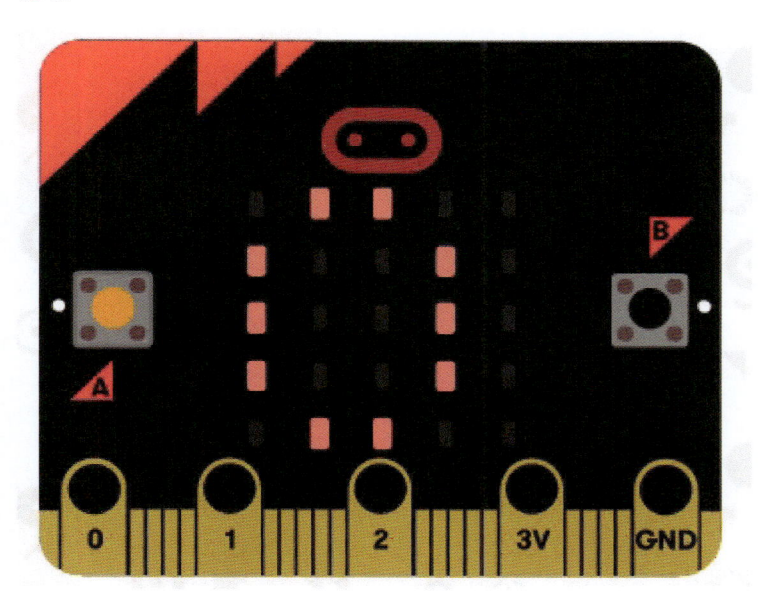

Next, we need to tell the Microbit what to do if the hook touches the maze. You are going to be connecting your hook to the '0' pin on the bottom of your Microbit and connecting your maze to the GND (ground) pin. We need to tell the Microbit that when it detects a connection at '0' it should show a cross, a sad face or a message and then increase the losses by 1.

First let's programme the system to show a picture if the hook touches the maze.

Go to input (purple) and select the 'on pin P0 pressed' command. Drag it to your screen below the 'on button A' pressed

Page | 57

commands from before so your screen looks like the image below.

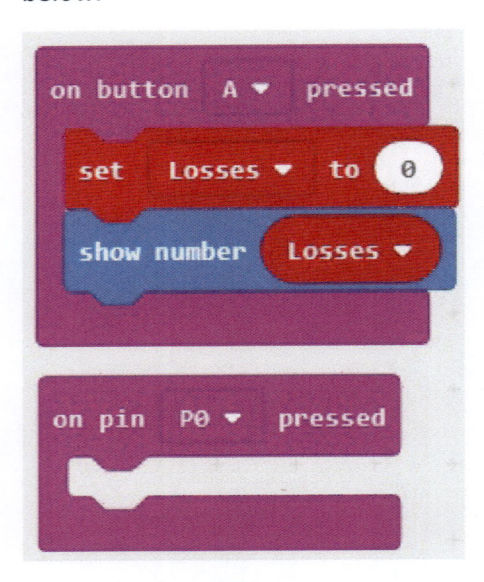

Next, go to the basic commands (blue) and select what you would like your Micro:bit to display if your hook touches your maze. You may write a short message using 'show string', use 'show leds' to show your own picture or choose one of the icons. You could even make a short animation by making a series of pictures like in our animation activity. We've gone for a cross icon below.

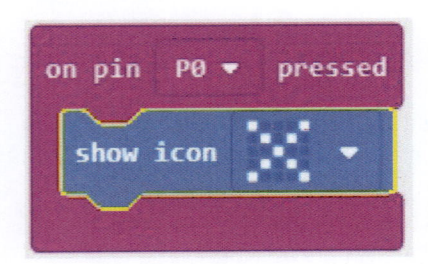

CODING

If you are using an image you will want it to stay on screen for a little while so you don't miss it. Go to the basic commands again (blue) and drag a pause command underneath the show icon or show LEDs command. This is how long you want your image to show for. We've gone for 100milliseconds

Finally, all we need to do is tell the system to add an extra loss on every time the hook touches the wire.

Click variables (red) and drag a 'change losses by 1' command below your pause command.

Page | 59

CODING

Finally, we need to tell the system to show the number of losses again every time the hook touches the maze. We did this right at the beginning. All you have to do is drag a 'show number' command from 'Basic' (blue) to underneath your 'change losses' command.

Your programme is now finished! Now you need to download it to your Microbit and then we can get started building the actual game itself.

Your Microbit has 25 gold pins. You can see them all in the picture below. Pins are places where other things can be connected to the Microbit such as wires, speakers, etc.

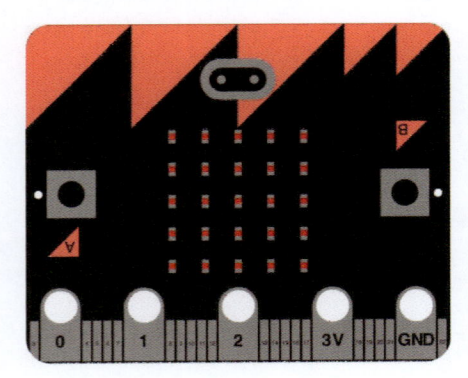

Page | 60

CODING

The five big holes are the ones we are going to focus on today as they are the pins that we can connect the alligator test leads to. 0, 1 and 2 can be used for lots of different things so are called general pins. 3V is a power supply. Your Microbit receives power from either the USB cable or the battery pack. It can then give some of this power out to other devices through the 3V pin so you don't need to power those other devices separately. This would be useful if you were attaching an amplified speaker to your Microbit.

GND means ground and is used to complete a circuit. In our wire following game, we programmed the Microbit to know when pin 0 is connected to the GND pin. You can test this with your body! Download the wire following game onto your Microbit and attach the battery pack. Press A to start the game then hold the GND pin with your right thumb and finger and touch the 0 pin with your left hand and then release it. Did you see your 'loss' animation/picture/word and see the number of losses go up? This is because electricity is going through your body and connecting the pin 0 to the ground pin. Don't worry, it's perfectly safe – you just had around 3V of electricity going through you – the same amount as if you pick up a 3V battery and touch both sides. It's not enough for you to even feel it! Don't worry if this doesn't work for you, it doesn't always work for everyone.

Next, let's turn that into a game.

WARNING – never connect the 3V and GND pins together because it can damage your Microbit.

Connect one end of one of your test leads to the 0 pin using the clip that looks a bit like an alligator's mouth. Connect one end of the other test lead to the GND pin like in the picture below. You may wish to slide the plastic cover off the clip to make it a bit easier. If you touch the other empty ends of the leads together, you should see your loss animation.

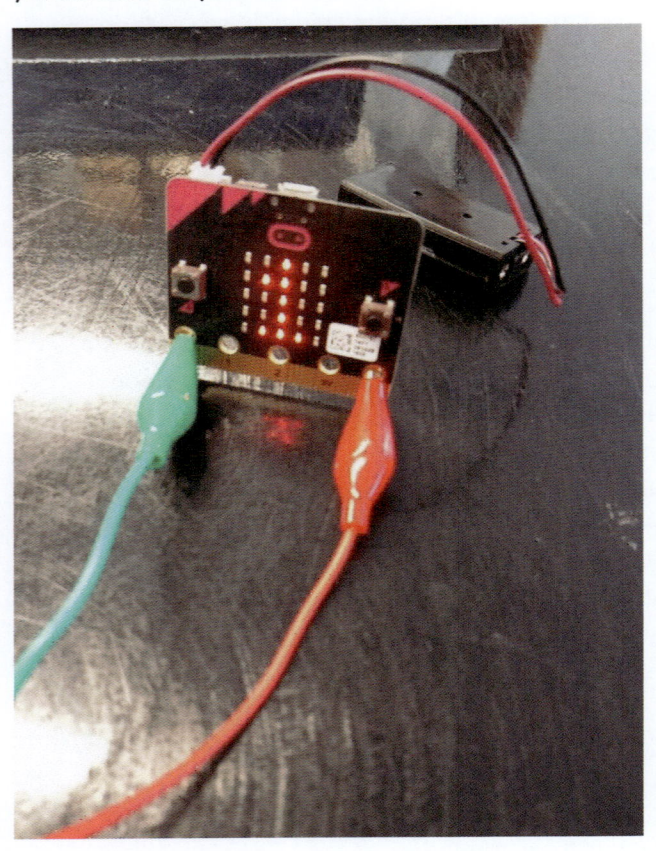

CODING

Now, with your long conductive wire, make a maze shape. Use blue tack or modelling clay to hold the wire up. Like this.

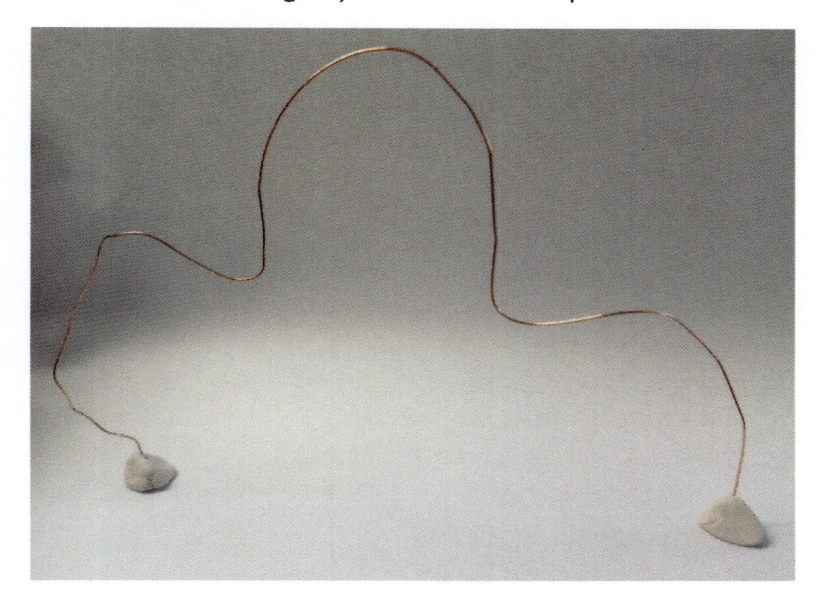

With the short conductive wire, make a small hook shape. This will be used to move around your maze so the smaller it is, the harder the game will be.

Take the end of the lead that is connected to the 0 pin and connect it to your maze.

Take the end of the lead that is connected to the GND pin and connect it to your hook. Like this.

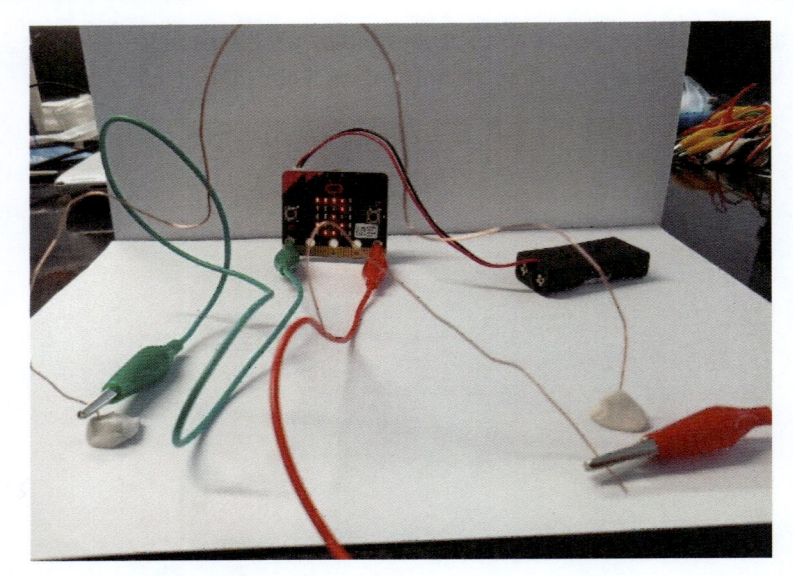

Now, you are ready to play. Take your hook and place it at the start of your maze. Move it along the whole maze, trying not to touch the maze. You may want to get someone to watch your Microbit's screen and tell you if you touch the maze. At the end of the maze, see how many losses you've had.

If it's too easy, try making the maze more bendy or making the hook smaller.

If you find the system is recording losses when you haven't touched the maze, it's likely something else is making the connection. Make sure you are working on a non-conductive surface. Some tables can conduct electricity so try putting your maze and Microbit on a piece of paper like in the picture above.

Challenge a friend and see if they can do it with less losses than you.

Activity 13 – Connecting a speaker to your Microbit

For this activity you will need:

Alligator test leads x 2

Piezo speaker

Microbit and battery pack

A piezo is very small and looks like this. They can be found very cheaply online. The two little metal legs are the places where you will connect it to your Microbit.

To connect your speaker to the Microbit you will need to take one of your alligator test leads and clip one end to one of the metal 'legs' on the speaker. Attach the other end of this lead to pin 0 on the Microbit.

Take the other alligator test lead and clip one end of it to the other metal leg on the speaker. Attach the other end of this lead to the GND pin on your Microbit. The complete circuit will look like this.

Now let's see if it works! Go to makecode.microbit.org and start a new project. Call it something like 'playing a tune'.

The system has a few pre-programmed tunes or you can compose your own tune. We are going to do both! To start with, get rid of the 'on-start' and 'forever' commands and get yourself an 'on button B pressed' command. Next, go to the 'music' menu and drag the command that says 'start melody dadadum repeating once' into the gap in the 'on button B pressed' command.

Page | 66

CODING

```
on button B ▼ pressed
    start melody  dadadum ▼  repeating  once ▼
```

'dadadum is the name of a song that is pre-programmed into the system. Press the B button on the simulator (on the left hand side) to hear what this sounds like. Make sure your computer has the volume turned up! If you click the arrow by 'dadadum' you can change the tune. Try a few and pick your favourite. This will play when you press button B.

Download your programme onto your Microbit, make sure your speaker is connected and press button B. Can you hear the tune you programmed?

Activity 14 – Composing a tune

The system can also be used to compose (create) your own music. Open back up your project from the last activity and drag an 'on button A pressed' command onto the screen and then go back to the music menu. Drag the 'play tone middle C for 1 beat' command into the gap in the 'on button A pressed' command. It will look like this…

CODING

```
on button A ▼ pressed
    play tone ( Middle C ) for ( 1 ▼ ) beat
```

Middle C is the name of a music note. If you click on 'middle C' you will see a picture of a piano keyboard come up. You can click on whichever note you would like the Microbit to play. You can also change where it says 'for 1 beat'. This is how long you want your note to go on for. 1/16 is the shortest note and 4 is the longest note. Here I have told the system to play Middle A for 1/4 beat.

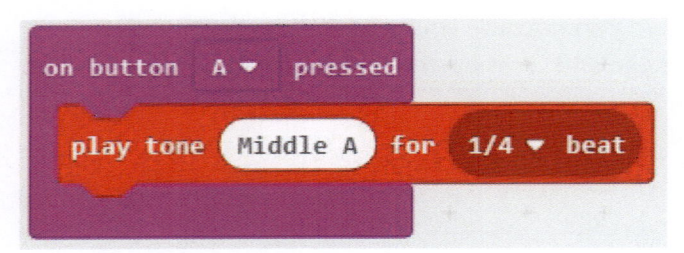

```
on button A ▼ pressed
    play tone ( Middle A ) for ( 1/4 ▼ ) beat
```

If we put lots of these commands together, the system will play them all in a row and that is how we can play a tune. You can put notes together in whichever order you like and then test out your tune in the simulator. Change the notes until you are happy with your tune. You can either make up your own tune, try and create a tune you have heard before or copy the blocks from the examples on the next few pages. When you are happy with your tune, download it onto your Microbit, make sure your speaker is connected, and then play your tune to everyone!

Everything is awesome

If you have ever watched the Lego Movie, you will know this song. Copy the commands below into your Makecode editor to have your Microbit play 'everything is awesome'.

```
on button A ▼ pressed
    play tone  Middle G#  for  1/2 ▼ beat
    play tone  Middle G#  for  1/2 ▼ beat
    play tone  Middle G#  for  1/2 ▼ beat
    play tone  Middle G#  for  1/2 ▼ beat
    play tone  Middle G#  for  1/2 ▼ beat
    play tone  Middle G   for  4 ▼ beat
    rest(ms)  1/2 ▼ beat
    play tone  Middle G#  for  1/2 ▼ beat
    play tone  Middle G#  for  1/2 ▼ beat
    play tone  Middle G#  for  1/2 ▼ beat
    play tone  Middle G#  for  1/2 ▼ beat
```

CODING

- play tone **Middle G#** for 1 beat
- play tone **Middle G** for 1/2 beat
- play tone **Middle F** for 1/2 beat
- play tone **Middle D#** for 1/2 beat
- play tone **Middle F** for 1/2 beat
- play tone **Middle G** for 1/2 beat
- play tone **Middle F** for 2 beat
- rest(ms) 1/2 beat
- play tone **Middle G#** for 1/2 beat
- play tone **Middle G#** for 1/2 beat
- play tone **Middle G#** for 1/2 beat
- play tone **Middle G#** for 1/2 beat

CODING

```
play tone (Middle G#) for (1/2 ▼) beat
play tone (Middle A#) for (4 ▼) beat
play tone (Low A#) for (1/2 ▼) beat
play tone (Low A#) for (1/2 ▼) beat
play tone (Middle G) for (1 ▼) beat
play tone (Middle F) for (1/2 ▼) beat
play tone (Middle F) for (1/2 ▼) beat
play tone (Middle D#) for (1/2 ▼) beat
play tone (Middle D#) for (4 ▼) beat
```

Happy birthday

Copy the commands below and on the next pages to make your Microbit play happy birthday.

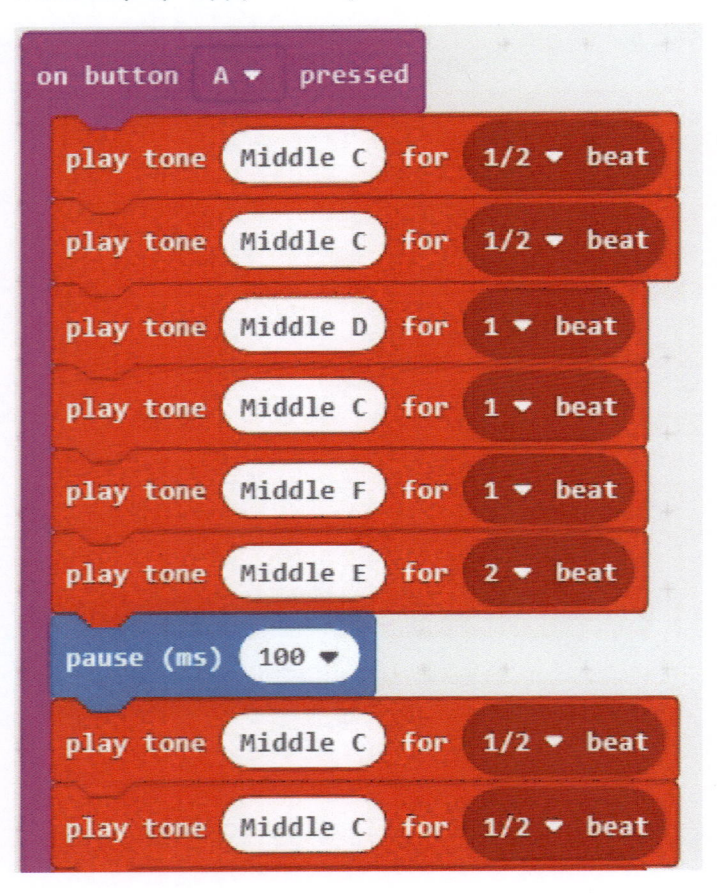

```
on button A pressed
    play tone Middle C for 1/2 beat
    play tone Middle C for 1/2 beat
    play tone Middle D for 1 beat
    play tone Middle C for 1 beat
    play tone Middle F for 1 beat
    play tone Middle E for 2 beat
    pause (ms) 100
    play tone Middle C for 1/2 beat
    play tone Middle C for 1/2 beat
```

Fun Science — CODING

```
play tone  Middle D   for  1 ▼ beat
play tone  Middle C   for  1 ▼ beat
play tone  Middle G   for  1 ▼ beat
play tone  Middle F   for  2 ▼ beat
pause (ms) 100 ▼
play tone  Middle C   for  1/2 ▼ beat
play tone  Middle C   for  1/2 ▼ beat
play tone  High C     for  1 ▼ beat
play tone  Middle A   for  1 ▼ beat
play tone  Middle F   for  1 ▼ beat
```

CODING

```
play tone  Middle E   for  1 ▼ beat
play tone  Middle D   for  2 ▼ beat
pause (ms)  100 ▼
play tone  Middle A#  for  1/2 ▼ beat
play tone  Middle A#  for  1/2 ▼ beat
play tone  Middle A   for  1 ▼ beat
play tone  Middle F   for  1 ▼ beat
play tone  Middle G   for  1 ▼ beat
play tone  Middle F   for  2 ▼ beat
```

Activity 15 – Making a tug of war game with sound!

In this activity, we are going to be making a virtual tug of war game on the Microbit's screen. There will be a light in the middle of the screen and pressing A will move the light closer to the A button. Pressing B will move the light closer to the B button. One player will press the A button really fast whilst the other player presses the B button really fast. If A presses the button the fastest, the light will move towards the A side. If B presses the button the fastest, the light will move to the B side. If the light gets all the way to one side, the Microbit will play a tune and the screen will tell you that either A or B has won.

You will need to connect your speaker up to your Microbit for the tunes to play so you can either do this now or after you've downloaded the code onto your Microbit.

Start a new project at makecode.microbit.org and name it something like 'tug of war'.

We actually need both the 'on start' and 'forever' commands so don't delete either of them! First, we need to tell the Microbit to start by putting a light in the middle of the screen. Do you remember the 'sprites' from the gaming menu? Sprites are moveable characters (or in this case lights) in a game. You may also remember our co-ordinates from when we made the reaction game. We can use co-ordinates to tell our system where to put a sprite. First, we need to go to the variables menu, make a new variable and call it 'sprite'. Drag the 'set sprite to 0' command and put it in the 'on start' command like this.

Fun Science — CODING

```
on start
    set Sprite ▼ to ( 0 )
```

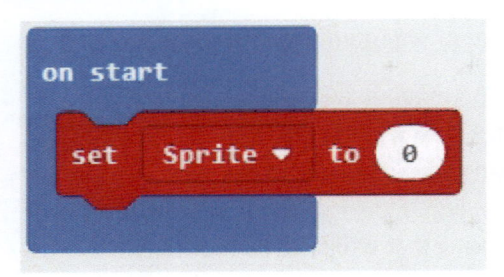

Next, we need to replace that 0 with a command from the gaming menu (underneath advanced). Drag the 'create sprite at x 2, y2' command to replace the 0 like this.

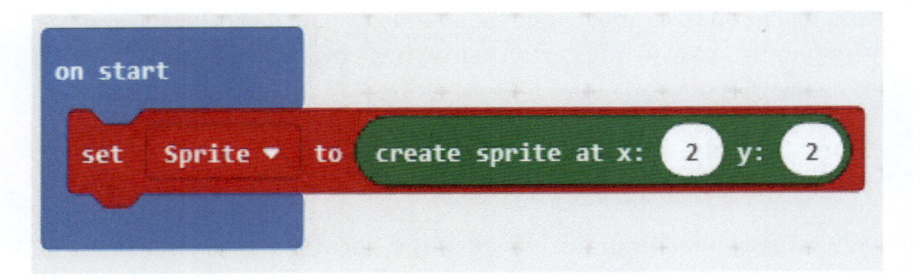

```
on start
    set Sprite ▼ to create sprite at x: 2 y: 2
```

Look at your simulator. Can you see a light right in the middle of the screen? That's the sprite! It's in the middle because that is 2,2. Take a look at the grid below and see if you can remember why the middle light is 2,2.

CODING

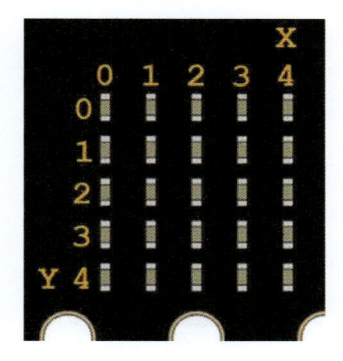

So, now we've put the light in the middle, we need to tell the system to move it in the direction of the A button when A is pressed and in the direction of the B button when B is pressed.

Go to the inputs menu and get an 'on button A pressed' command. Next, go to the gaming menu and get a 'sprite change x by 1' command and put it in your 'on button A pressed' block. Like this

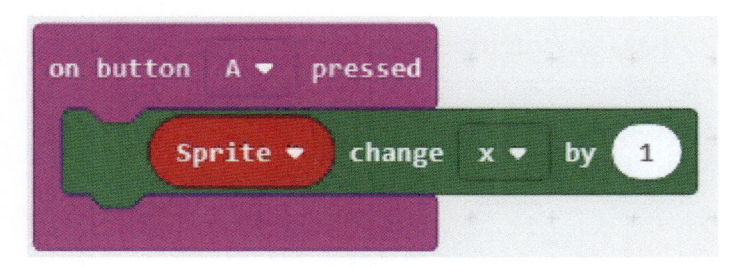

This tells the system that when A is pressed, the x value of the sprite is going to go up by one. This means it will change from two to three. Try it in your simulator. What do you notice? It's going in the wrong direction! We want the light to move towards A when A is pressed. Change the 1 to -1 and try the simulator again. That's better! The only problem is, the game will be over

Page | 77

quite quickly like this because it will only take two clicks of the button for A to win. They could win before B is even ready! So, we are going to change the number to -0.1. Like this.

on button A pressed
Sprite change x by -0.1

This means that you actually have to press the A button 10 times to get the light to move one 'jump' towards the A. Give this a go!

Now, let's do a similar thing for the B button. You can either duplicate this whole block (right click on the 'on button A pressed' command and click duplicate) or you can go back to the input menu and get an 'on button B pressed' command then go to the gaming menu and get another 'sprite change x by 1' command. This time, we want the number to be 0.1 because we want the light to move towards the B button when B is pressed. It should look like this.

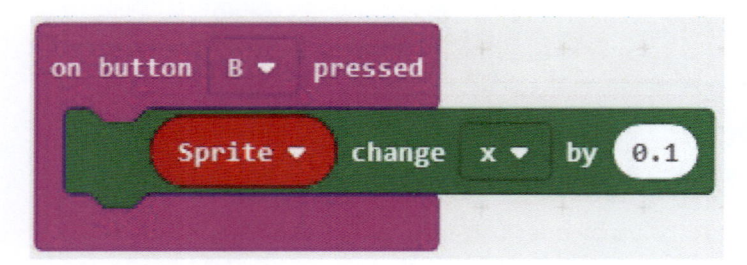

on button B pressed
Sprite change x by 0.1

Give it a go in the simulator. Remember that nothing will seem to happen until you've pressed one of the buttons 10 times but the system is counting the clicks!

CODING

Finally, we need to tell the system what to do when A wins and what to do when B wins. Find your forever block and then go to the logic menu and get an 'if true then _____ else if true then_____' command and put it inside your forever block. Click the bottom plus and then click the bottom minus until you get something that looks like this.

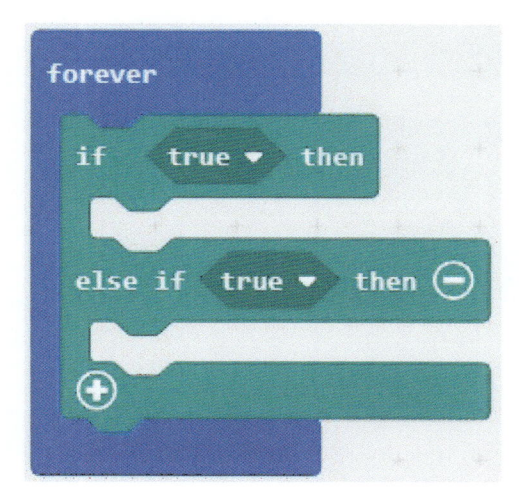

Go back to the logic menu and drag a '0 = 0' command to replace the first 'true' like this.

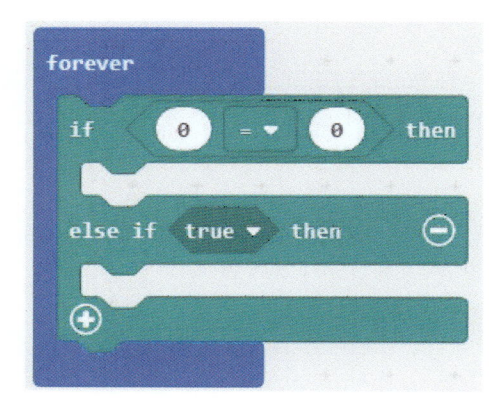

Now we need to replace the first 0 with a 'sprite x' command from the game menu. Like this.

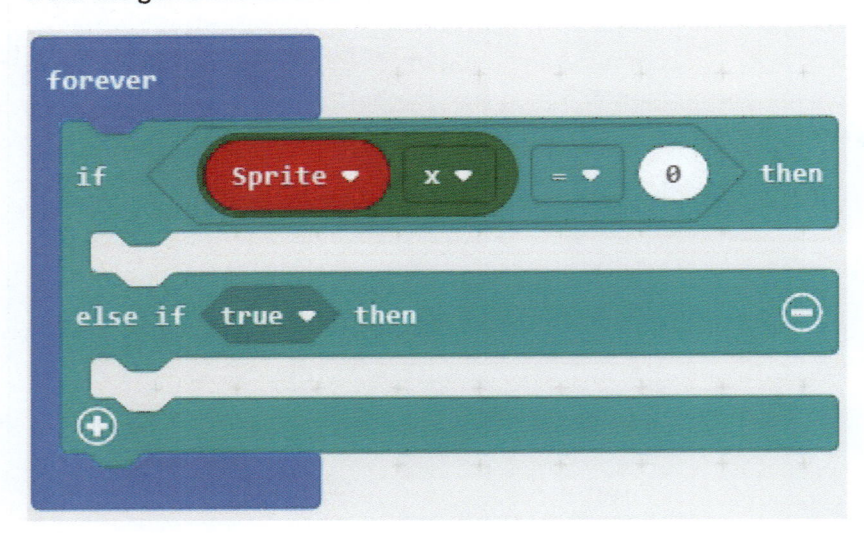

This tells the system that if the sprite is in the position circled below, it needs to do something.

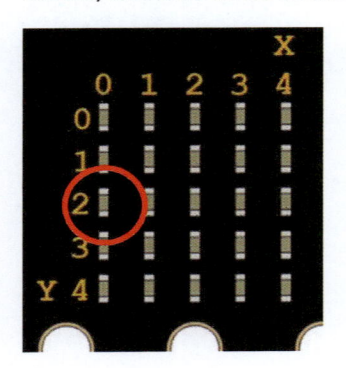

If the light reaches this position, it means that A has won because the light has moved towards the A button. When A wins, we want the system to play a tune and then tell us that A has won. Let's programme that now. Go to the music menu and drag

Page | 80

a 'start melody 'dadadum repeating once' command to underneath the 'if sprite x = 0' command. Like this.

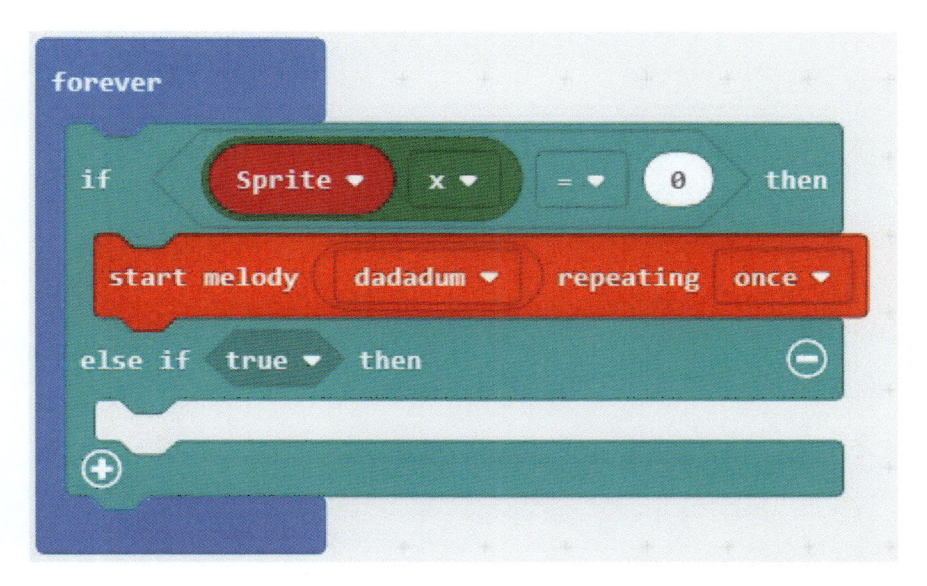

```
forever
    if  Sprite ▼  x ▼    = ▼   0   then
        start melody  dadadum ▼  repeating  once ▼
    else if  true ▼  then                        ⊖

    ⊕
```

Use the arrow next to dadadum to change the tune to whatever you like best.

We also want the screen to tell us that A has won. Grab a 'show string hello' command and put it underneath your 'start melody...' command. Change the word 'hello' to 'A wins'. Like this.

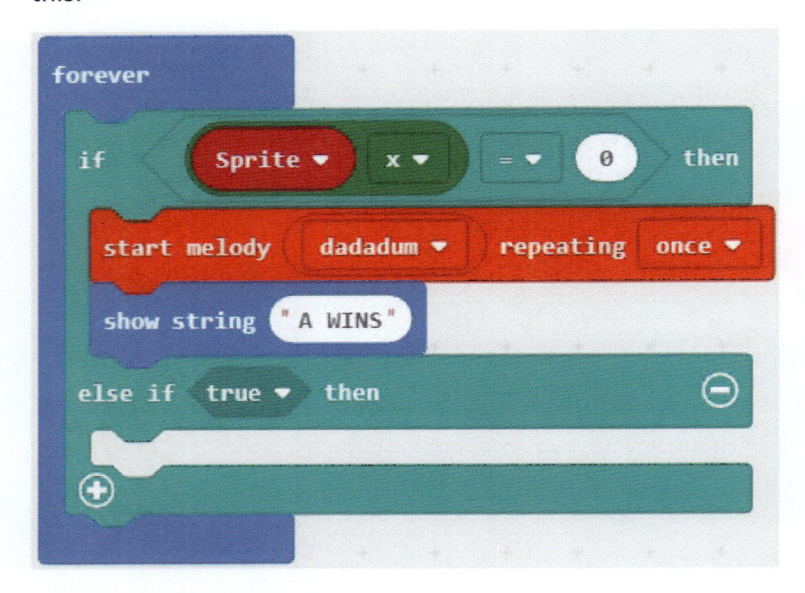

```
forever
    if  Sprite ▼  x ▼  = ▼  0  then
        start melody  dadadum ▼  repeating  once ▼
        show string  "A WINS"
    else if  true ▼  then
```

Test your code with the simulator. Press the A button lots of times and see what happens! The system will keep repeating the tune and 'A wins' because we haven't yet told it to reset the game. Don't worry about that for now.

Now we need to do the same for if B wins. Just like before, go to the logic menu and drag an 'if 0=0' command to replace 'true' then replace the first 0 with 'sprite x' from the game menu. Like this.

Page | 82

CODING

We need to change that second 0 to a 4 because B wins when the light gets to this position.

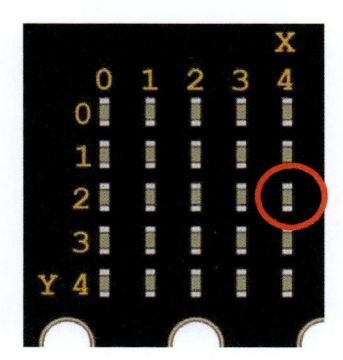

Next, we need to choose a different tune to play when B wins. Grab a 'start melody dadadum' command from the music menu and put it in place like this. I've changed my melody to be 'power up' but you can choose whatever you like.

Page | 83

```
forever
  if  Sprite ▼  x ▼  = ▼  0  then
    start melody  dadadum ▼  repeating  once ▼
    show string  "A WINS"
  else if  Sprite ▼  x ▼  = ▼  0  then ⊖
    start melody  power up ▼  repeating  once ▼
  ⊕
```

Next, we need the screen to tell us that B has won. Get a 'show string hello' command from the basic menu and drag it into place like this. Change the words to B WINS.

```
forever
  if  Sprite ▼  x ▼  = ▼  0  then
    start melody  dadadum ▼  repeating  once ▼
    show string  "A WINS"
  else if  Sprite ▼  x ▼  = ▼  0  then ⊖
    start melody  power up ▼  repeating  once ▼
    show string  "B WINS"
  ⊕
```

Finally, we just need to make sure that, no matter who wins, the system puts the light back in the middle ready for another game and doesn't keep playing the tune and saying that A or B has won! Underneath 'show string A wins', put a 'sprite set x to 0' command from the game menu and change the 0 to a 2. Like this.

```
forever
    if  Sprite ▼  x ▼  = ▼  0  then
        start melody  dadadum ▼  repeating  once ▼
        show string  "A WINS"
        Sprite ▼  set  x ▼  to  2
    else if  Sprite ▼  x ▼  = ▼  0  then ⊖
        start melody  power up ▼  repeating  once ▼
        show string  "B WINS"
    ⊕
```

Do exactly the same underneath 'show string B wins'. The final code should look like this.

Download your code onto your Microbit, make sure your speaker is connected, and challenge someone to a battle!

<u>Activity 16 – Making a circuit with a breadboard</u>

For this activity you will need:

Alligator test leads x 4

Breadboard jump wires x 4 (these are the thin, coloured wires)

RGB LED (Looks like a little light. Also known as a Red, Green, Blue, Light Emitting Diode – this is a type of component that can light up in three different colours or a mixture of those colours)

100 ohm resistor x 3 (this is another type of component. They look like little brown cylinders with a wire coming out of each end)

CODING

Breadboard. Your breadboard may look a bit like this.

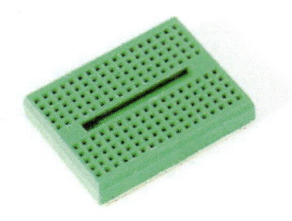

...but it may be a different colour and it may be a bit bigger.

Breadboards are used for making complicated circuits. We could use alligator leads or wires instead but the whole thing would get very messy and complicated! Electricians and scientists use breadboards to test things really easily.

On top of your breadboard are 170 holes called pins. You can push electrical wires and components (like a resistor or an LED) into these holes and they will stay there.

Underneath your breadboard, some of the holes are connected in rows. Like this.

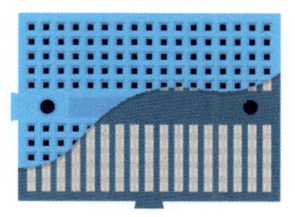

This means that we can put wires into one hole and the breadboard will connect them to other wires in the same row. Can you see the green squares in the picture below? These are all connected because they are in the same row. Don't worry if this all feels a bit confusing! Hopefully it will get easier when we start adding our components.

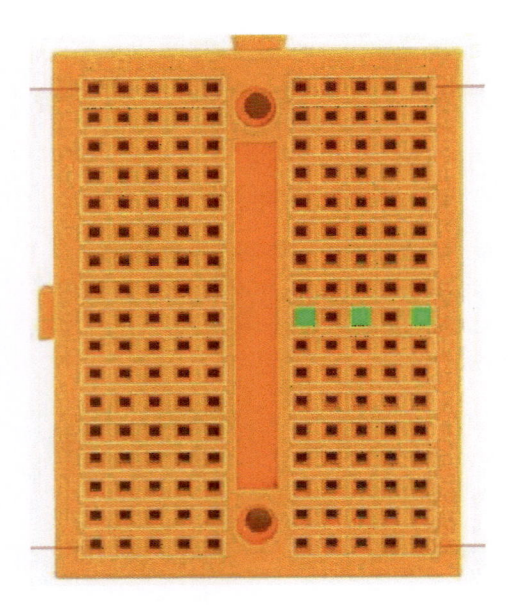

Components just means 'things that are going in our circuit'. Let's try putting some components into our breadboard. Copy the pictures and instructions below and see if you can copy my circuit.

Take your LED. Can you see that it has 4 'legs' and one is longer than the others? Put it into your breadboard like in the picture below. The short legs should go where the green squares are and the long leg where the red square is.

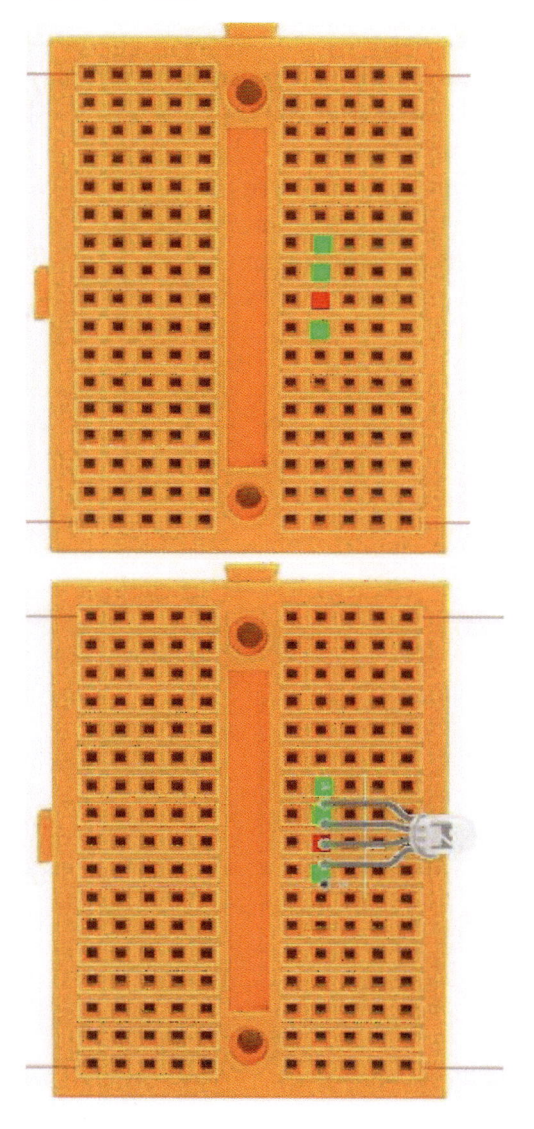

CODING

CODING

Next, we need to put in the resistors. Resistors reduce the amount of power going to the LED. LEDs don't need much power to work so we use a resistor to 'slow down' the power going to them from the Microbit. Take your three resistors and put them across the gap in the middle of the breadboard like in the picture. They should be in the same rows as the short legs of the LED. Copy the diagram below. The resistors in the picture below are blue so you can see them easily but yours are brown and stripey.

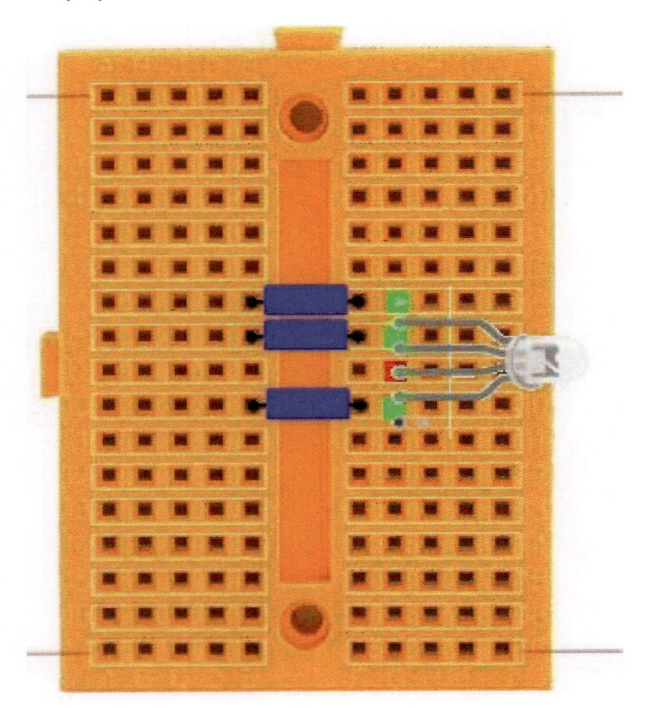

Next you need to get your four jumper wires. You need to put one end of each wire into the squares marked in pink on the diagram below. We've squashed the LED in the diagram below so that you can see where to put the wires!

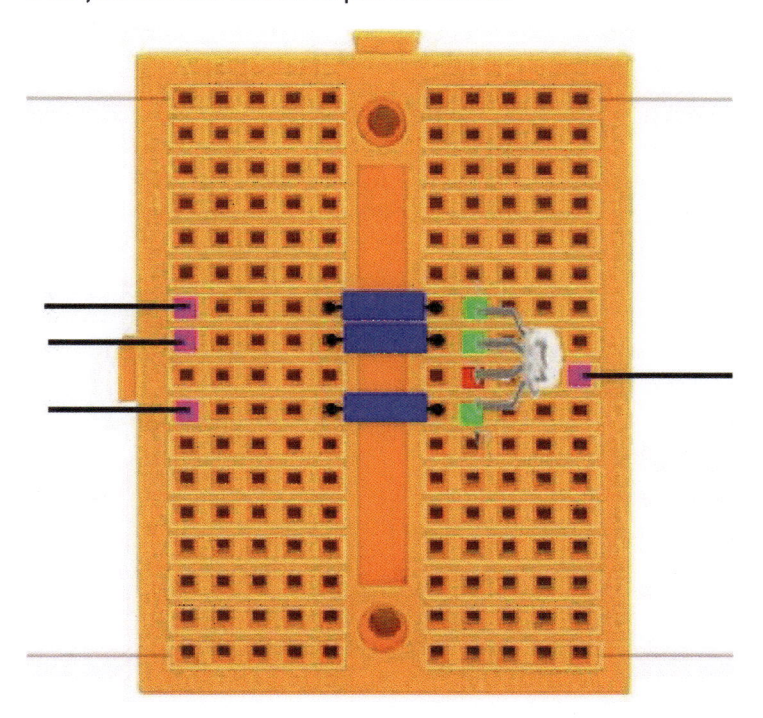

Now we just have to connect all of that up to the Microbit. You may have noticed that three of the wires (on the left hand side in the diagram) are in the same rows as the ones with resistors in and also the rows with the short legs of the LED in. The other wire (on the right hand side) is in the same row as the long leg of the LED.

Take three of your alligator test leads and attach them to the three wires on the left hand side. One test lead per wire. Like this.

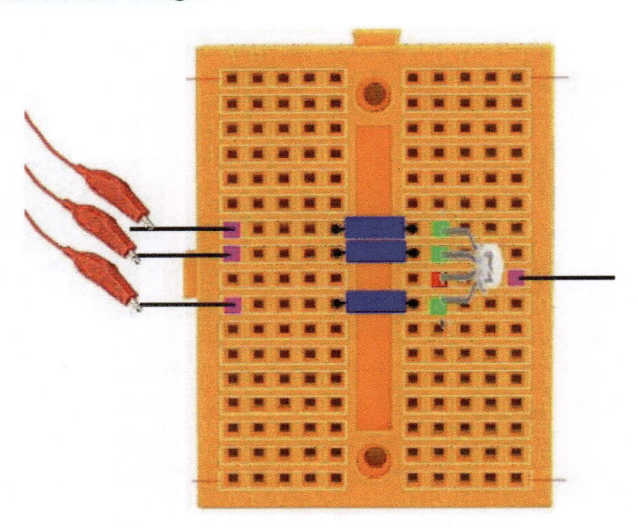

Take your other alligator test lead and attach it to the wire on the right hand side.

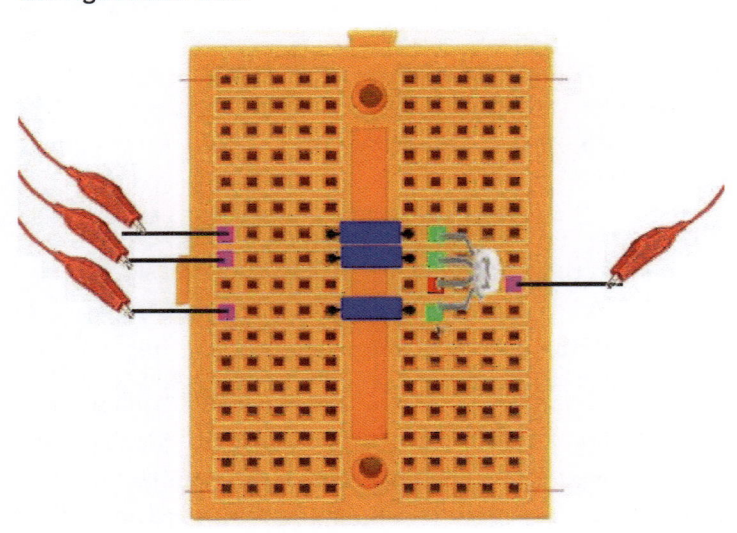

CODING

Now we are ready to attach the Microbit. In the diagram below I've given each clip a colour.

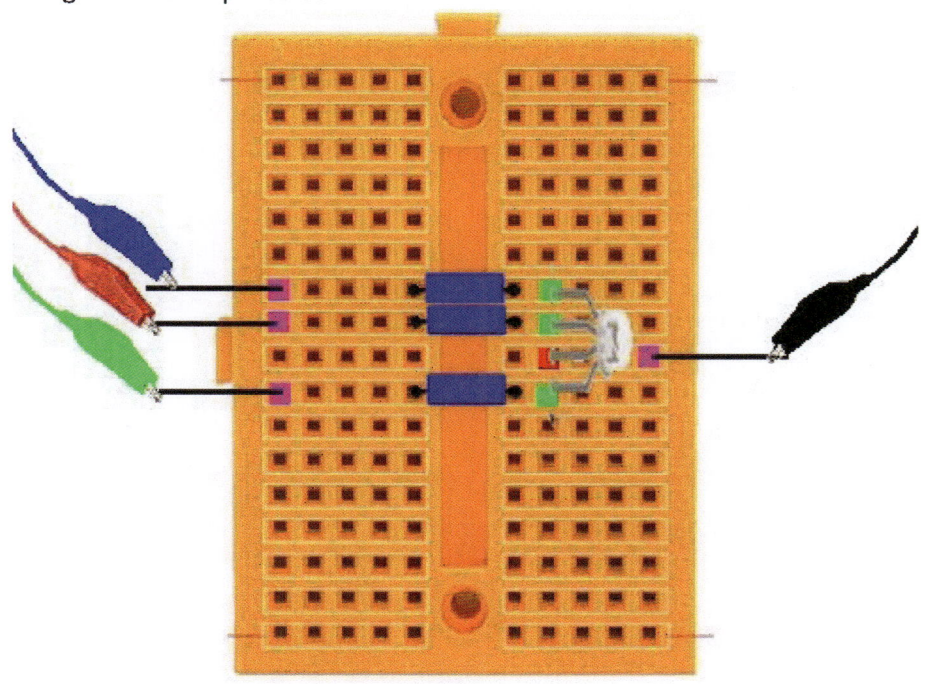

Your clips may be different colours.

You need to attach the other end of the clip coloured green in the diagram to the hole with a 0 by it on your Microbit.

You need to attach the other end of the clip coloured red in the diagram to the hole with a 1 by it.

You need to attach the other end of the clip coloured blue in the diagram to the hole with a 2 by it.

You need to attach the other end of the clip coloured black in the diagram to the hole with GND by it.

The whole thing should look like this.

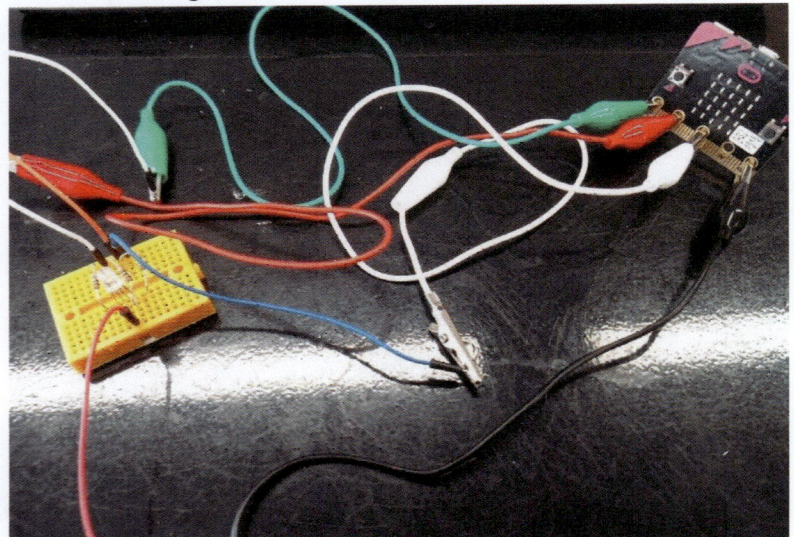

It looks a bit confusing doesn't it! Go back through the instructions and just double check that everything is in the right place. Remember, if you aren't sure, you can always watch our videos at:

www.fun-science.org.uk/bigboxofcodingvideos

Activity 17 – Making the primary colours of light

Now you've connected up a circuit with your LED light we need to find out whether it's working so we're going to be coding something to show us a different colour light, depending on which button we press. Start a new project by going to makecode.microbit.org and call it 'making a primary colour'.

Your LED actually has three lights inside it – red, green and blue. These are the primary colours of light. Normally when we talk about colours, we think of the primary colours as being red, yellow and blue. These are the primary colours of paint or ink but when we're talking about light, the primary colours are red, green and blue. Your circuit has been made so that the green light is connected to pin 0, the red light is connected to pin 1 and the blue light is connected to pin 2.

First, get rid of the 'on-start' and 'forever' commands and then drag an 'on button A pressed' command onto your screen from the purple input menu. Like this.

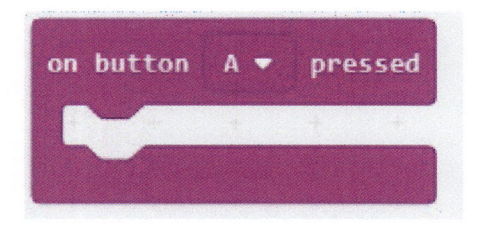

Next, we're going to be using a new menu, which is the pins menu. You can find it by clicking the black 'advanced' button which is in the middle of the screen near the bottom. This then shows you lots of new menus. Scroll down and click on 'pins'.

Fun Science — CODING

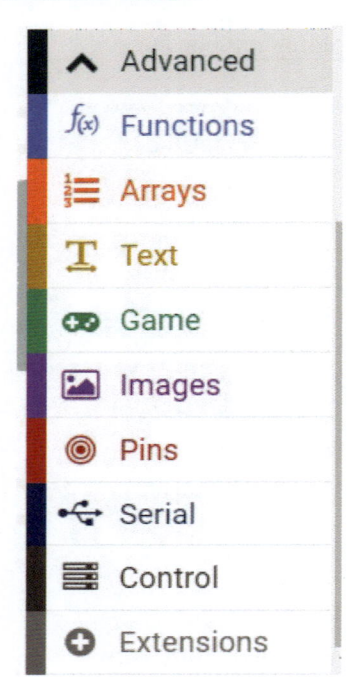

- Advanced
- Functions
- Arrays
- Text
- Game
- Images
- Pins
- Serial
- Control
- Extensions

In this menu you will see lots of things that might look like very strange words! We've got 'digital write pin', 'analog read pin', 'analog write pin' etc. One difference between the words digital and analog is that if something is digital, it's either on or off, there's no in-between. Something analog can be on, off or somewhere between like half on! For now, we are going to be using the 'digital write pin' so that we can turn our different colours of light on and off. Later, in another activity, we are going to use the analog commands.

Click and drag the 'digital write pin p0 to 0' command and place it inside the 'on button A pressed' command. Like this.

CODING

```
on button A ▼ pressed
    digital write pin P0 ▼ to 0
```

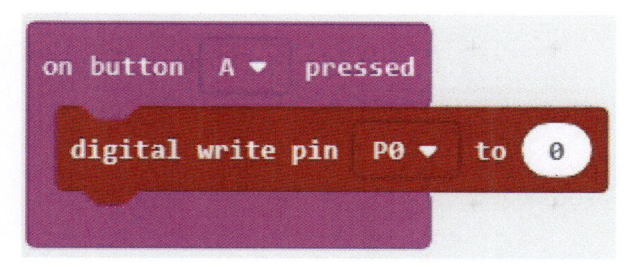

This tells the system that pin P0 (where our green light is connected) is 0 which means off. Change this number to 1. In digital systems, 0 means off and 1 means on.

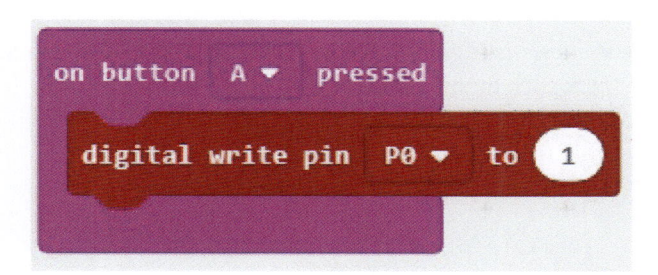

```
on button A ▼ pressed
    digital write pin P0 ▼ to 1
```

This command basically tells the system whether to send power to that pin or not. We've now told the system 'when we press button A, send power to the green light' which will turn the green light on. We are now going to do the same for pins P1 and P2. You can save time by right clicking on 'digital write pin P0 to 1' and clicking 'duplicate' or you can just get another `digital write pin P0 ▼ to 0` command from the pins menu. Put this underneath the first digital write pin P0 to 1 command and change P0 to P1 using the arrow by the P0 so you end up with something like this.

CODING

```
on button  A ▼  pressed
    digital write pin  P0 ▼  to  1
    digital write pin  P1 ▼  to  0
```

We've now told the system that, when button A is pressed, it should not send any power to pin P1 which is where the red light is connected. So there will be no red light. Do exactly the same thing again (either by right clicking and duplicating or by getting another command from the pins menu) and change P1 to P2 so you get something like this.

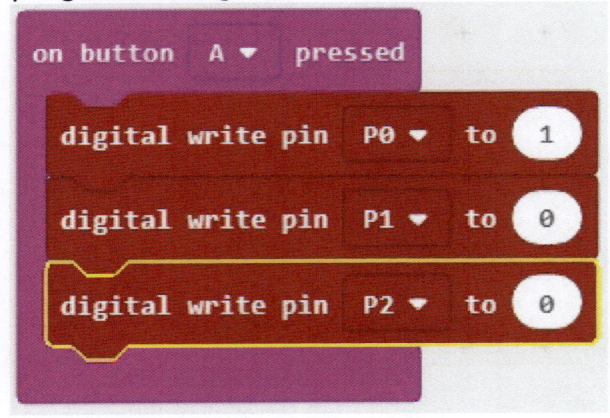

```
on button  A ▼  pressed
    digital write pin  P0 ▼  to  1
    digital write pin  P1 ▼  to  0
    digital write pin  P2 ▼  to  0
```

So, now, we have told the system that when button A is pressed, it should send power to the green light and not send any power to the red light or the blue light. This should mean that the light shows up as green.

CODING

Now, let's programme in the other lights. Right click on the 'on button A pressed' command and click duplicate. This will copy the whole command including the 'digital write pin' commands. The command will appear grey because you can't have two 'on button A pressed' commands on the screen. Change 'on button A pressed' to 'on button B pressed' so it looks like this.

```
on button B pressed
    digital write pin P0 to 1
    digital write pin P1 to 0
    digital write pin P2 to 0
```

At the moment, this command is exactly the same as the 'on button A pressed command' so we would get another green light if we press the B button. That's not very interesting so we need to tell the system to stop sending power to the green light (P0) and send power to the red light (P1) instead. Change the number in 'digital write pin P0' to 0 and change the number in 'digital write pin P1' to 1. Like this.

Page | 99

Fun Science — CODING

```
on button B ▼ pressed
    digital write pin P0 ▼ to 0
    digital write pin P1 ▼ to 1
    digital write pin P2 ▼ to 0
```

Finally, let's set button A+B to turn on the blue light. Right click on the 'on button B' pressed command and duplicate it. Again, it will be grey until you change the A to 'A+B' like this.

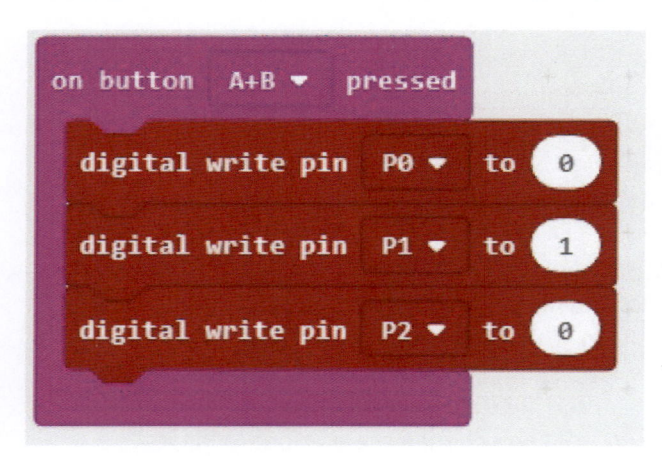

```
on button A+B ▼ pressed
    digital write pin P0 ▼ to 0
    digital write pin P1 ▼ to 1
    digital write pin P2 ▼ to 0
```

Finally, we just need to tell the system that, when A+B are pressed, we want it to stop sending power to the red light (P1) and send it to the blue light (P2). Change the number in 'digital write pin P1' to 0 and change the number in 'digital write pin P2' to 1. Like this.

Fun Science   CODING

```
on button  A+B ▼  pressed
    digital write pin  P0 ▼  to  0
    digital write pin  P1 ▼  to  0
    digital write pin  P2 ▼  to  1
```

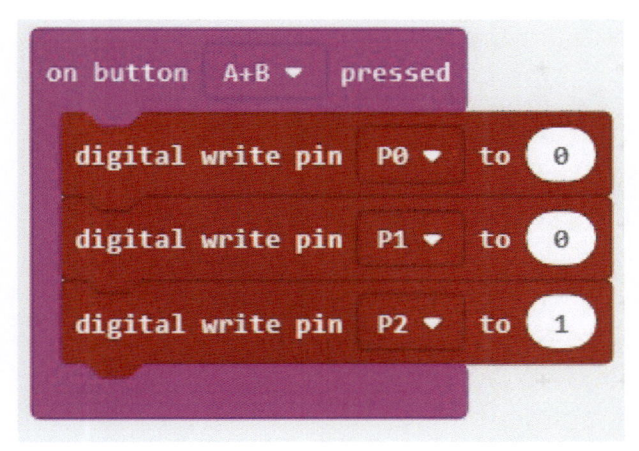

Download your project and copy it over to your Microbit. Make sure your circuit is all connected up and then try pressing A, B and A+B to see if you see all three colours. If it doesn't work, you can watch the troubleshooting video, which will show you all sorts of things that may have gone wrong with your circuit to try and help you to fix it.

Activity 18 – Making the secondary colours of light

Now you know that your light circuit works we are going to make some secondary colours. These are made by mixing colours of light. Remember, the primary colours of light are red, green and blue. From these colours we can get any colour of light that we like!

Go to makecode.microbit.org and load up your 'primary colours' project from the last activity. It should look like this.

Fun Science — CODING

```
on button A ▼ pressed
    digital write pin P0 ▼ to 1
    digital write pin P1 ▼ to 0
    digital write pin P2 ▼ to 0
```

```
on button A+B ▼ pressed
    digital write pin P0 ▼ to 0
    digital write pin P1 ▼ to 0
    digital write pin P2 ▼ to 1
```

```
on button B ▼ pressed
    digital write pin P0 ▼ to 0
    digital write pin P1 ▼ to 1
    digital write pin P2 ▼ to 0
```

In all of these commands, we are telling the system to send power to only one of the three lights. To make secondary colours we just need to send power to two of these lights at a time. Change your numbers so that in the 'on button A pressed' command you set pin P0 **and** pin P1 to 1. Like this.

```
on button A ▼ pressed
    digital write pin P0 ▼ to 1
    digital write pin P1 ▼ to 1
    digital write pin P2 ▼ to 0
```

Change your numbers so that in the 'on button B pressed' command you set pin P1 and P2 to 1. Like this.

```
on button B pressed
    digital write pin P0 to 0
    digital write pin P1 to 1
    digital write pin P2 to 1
```

Finally, change your numbers so that in the 'on button A+B pressed' command you set pin P0 and pin P1 to 1. Like this.

```
on button A+B pressed
    digital write pin P0 to 1
    digital write pin P1 to 0
    digital write pin P2 to 1
```

That's it! You've now created the three secondary colours of light (cyan, magenta and yellow). Download your programme onto your Microbit and give it a go. If you hold your hand or a piece of paper close to your LED you can see the two colours that are switched on. If you move your hand further away or just look at the LED from a distance you will see the colour that those two lights make when they are mixed together. Some of them may surprise you!

Activity 19 - Making more colours

Now we have explored the primary and secondary colours of light, we are going to try and create some different colours. By adjusting the amount of red, green and blue light, we can create any colour in the world. Web developers use this idea to create colours on websites and they call it a RGB value (red, green, blue).

Go to makecode.microbit.org and load up your 'secondary colours' project from the last activity. It should look like this.

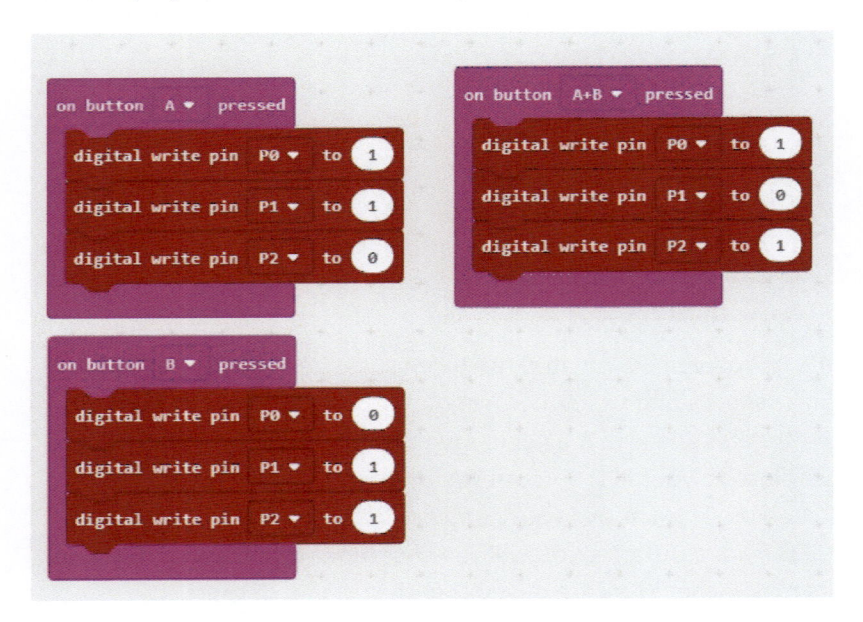

We learned earlier that something digital is either off (0) or on (1). In this activity we want to be able to switch the lights

CODING

partially on so we will need to use analog commands instead. Delete all the 'digital write pin...' commands and replace them with 'analogue write pin...' commands. You will find the 'analogue write pin...' command in the pins menu (remember it's hidden under advanced) and they will all automatically be set to 1023 to begin with which means fully switched on. Your screen should look like this when you are done.

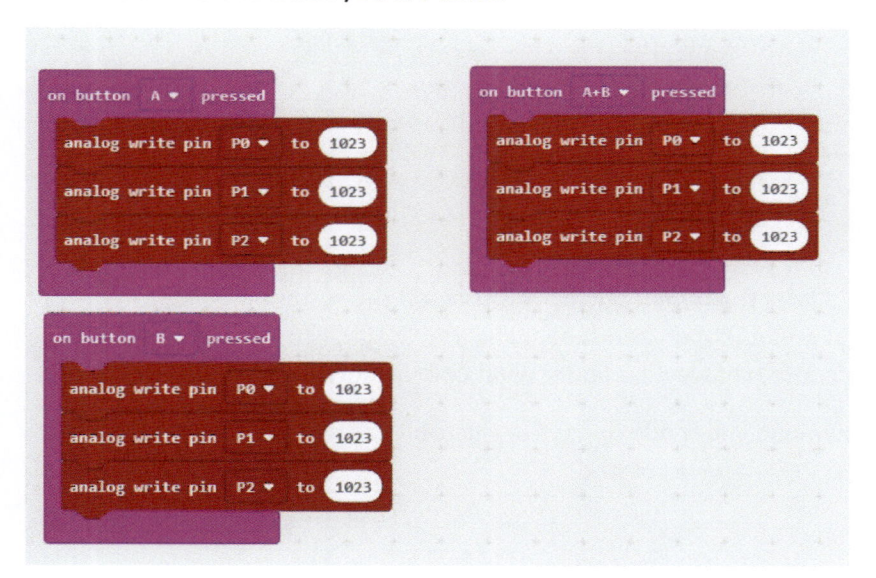

```
on button A ▾ pressed
    analog write pin P0 ▾ to 1023
    analog write pin P1 ▾ to 1023
    analog write pin P2 ▾ to 1023

on button A+B ▾ pressed
    analog write pin P0 ▾ to 1023
    analog write pin P1 ▾ to 1023
    analog write pin P2 ▾ to 1023

on button B ▾ pressed
    analog write pin P0 ▾ to 1023
    analog write pin P1 ▾ to 1023
    analog write pin P2 ▾ to 1023
```

At the moment, all the commands are the same and all the lights are set to fully on. If you have the red, green and blue lights all fully on they will all mix together to make white light.

If you click in one of the places where it says '1023' you will see a slider appear. If you slide this fully down to the left, the light will be fully off. If you put it in the middle, the light will be half on. Move your sliders around to mix up the numbers a bit. Below is what mine looks like but you don't need to copy my code, you can come up with your own numbers!

CODING

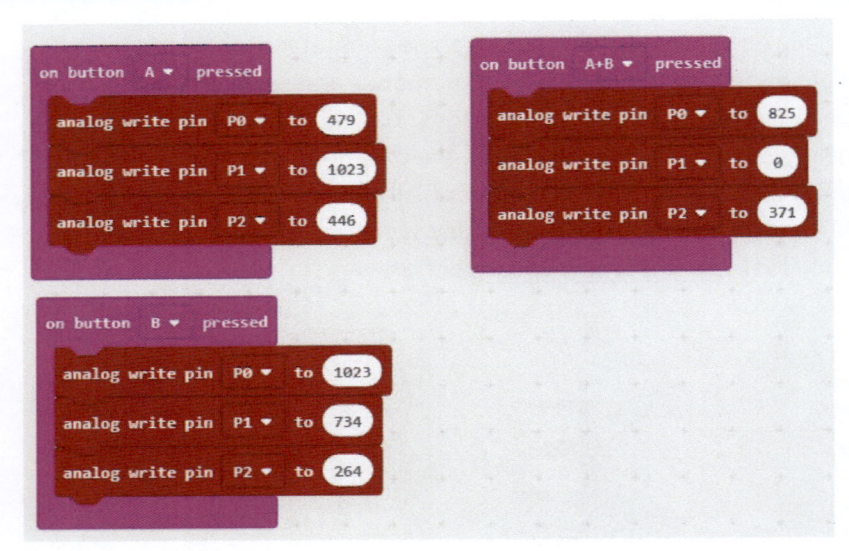

```
on button A ▼ pressed
    analog write pin P0 ▼ to 479
    analog write pin P1 ▼ to 1023
    analog write pin P2 ▼ to 446
```

```
on button A+B ▼ pressed
    analog write pin P0 ▼ to 825
    analog write pin P1 ▼ to 0
    analog write pin P2 ▼ to 371
```

```
on button B ▼ pressed
    analog write pin P0 ▼ to 1023
    analog write pin P1 ▼ to 734
    analog write pin P2 ▼ to 264
```

You'll see that when button A is pressed the system is going to turn green (P0) on about half way, red (P1) fully on and blue (P2) on about half way. I wonder what colour that will make!

Download your code onto your Microbit and see which three colours you have created!

Activity 20 - Making a random light generator.

This project is going to let the system decide how much power to send to each of the three pins so that you can press a button and get a random colour of light.

Start by going to makecode.microbit.org and starting a new project. Call this project something like 'random light generator'. You won't need the 'on start' command so you can get rid of this one but keep the 'forever' command.

For this project, we are going to start by making three variables and calling them green, red and blue.

Start by clicking the 'variables' menu and clicking 'create a variable'. Call this variable 'green'. Do this twice more until you've created green, blue and red. Like this.

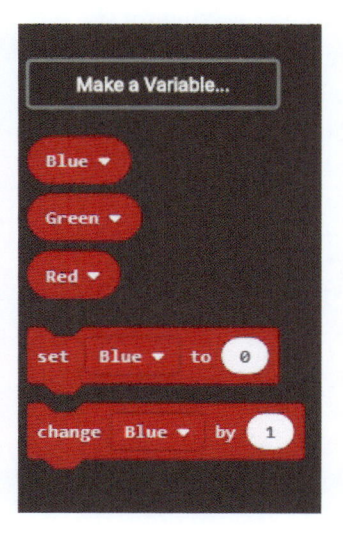

Page | 107

Now we need to 'define' the variables which means telling the system what they mean.

Remember, green is the light attached to P0, red is the light attached to P1 and blue is the light attached to P2. We know that but the system doesn't know that yet. Go over to the pins menu (hidden under the advanced button) and drag an 'analog write pin P0 to 1023' command to the gap in the 'forever' command. Like this.

Remember, we aren't actually going to be deciding on how bright our green light is, the system is going to be deciding for us. So we aren't going to put a number in where that 1023 is. Instead, we are going to replace that 1023 with the 'green' command from under the variables menu. So it looks like this.

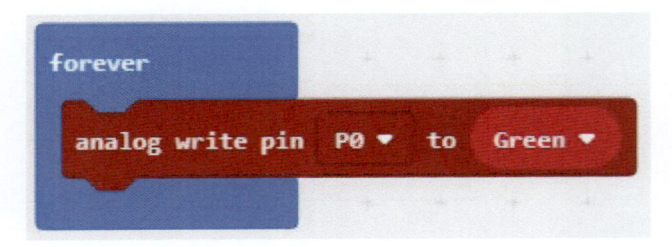

This is us defining the variable. We are telling the system that pin P0 is connected to the green light. If your pin P0 is connected to a different colour (e.g. red) set this as 'analog write pin P0 to red'.

Next, drag another 'analog write pin P0 to 1023' command to underneath the 'analog write pin P0 to green' command. Change P0 to P1 and drag the red command from the 'variables' menu to replace the 1023 number. So it looks like this.

Next, do exactly the same thing for blue. Either copy one of your 'analog write pin...' commands by right clicking it and clicking 'duplicate' or get another one from the pins menu. Change the P1 to P2 and get the 'blue' command from the variables menu and put it in place so that it looks like this.

That's it! We've defined our variables. Next, we need to create the piece of code that will make a random light.

Get yourself an 'on button A pressed' command from the inputs menu and drag it to somewhere on your screen. Next, go to the variables menu and drag a 'set green to 0' command into the 'on button A pressed' command. If you can only see a 'set blue to 0' or 'set red to 0' command then drag this one onto the screen and then use the arrow next to the colour to change the colour to green. It should look like this.

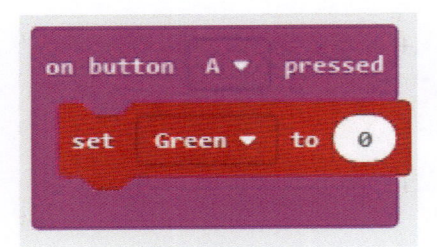

If we left it like this, when we press button A, the system will set the green light to 0 which means it would be switched off completely. We want the system to set this to a number between 0 and 1023 but we want it to decide which number on it's own. Go to the math menu and scroll down until you find this command.

Click and drag this command to replace the 0 in 'set green to 0' like this.

Page | 110

```
on button A ▼ pressed
    set Green ▼ to  pick random 0 to 10
```

We then need to change that 10 to 1023 because we know this is the maximum amount of power that we can send to the green light. So now, when we press the A button, the system will send a random amount of power to the green light. It may choose to completely switch it off, completely switch it on or somewhere inbetween.

Repeat the last two steps for red and blue until you end up with something that looks like this.

```
on button A ▼ pressed
    set Green ▼ to  pick random 0 to 1023
    set Red ▼ to  pick random 0 to 1023
    set Blue ▼ to  pick random 0 to 1023
```

That's it! You've created a random light generator.

When you press the A button, the system will send a random amount of electricity to each colour of light and they will mix together to create a random colour. If you press A again, it will send a different amount of electricity to each pin and create a different colour. You can keep pressing A and getting different colours.

Download your code onto your Microbit and enjoy creating random colours by pressing the A button!

Activity 21 – Generating colour codes

This next bit of code is going to make the screen of the Microbit tell you exactly what amounts of power it chose for each of the three colours. So, for example, if your Microbit had chosen to give 1023 units of power to green (fully switched on), 0 units of power to red (fully switched off) and 300 units of power to blue (roughly 1/3 switched on) you would see 1023 then 0 then 300 scroll across the screen. We can call this the 'colour code'.

Open up your random light generator code from the last activity so that we can add in the colour code generator.

To add this code, go to the basic menu and drag a 'show number 0' command to underneath your 'set blue to pick random 0 to 1023' command. Like this.

CODING

```
on button A ▼ pressed
    set Green ▼ to pick random 0 to 1023
    set Red ▼ to pick random 0 to 1023
    set Blue ▼ to pick random 0 to 1023
    show number 0
```

Go into the variables menu and drag a 'green' command to replace the 0. Like this.

```
on button A ▼ pressed
    set Green ▼ to pick random 0 to 1023
    set Red ▼ to pick random 0 to 1023
    set Blue ▼ to pick random 0 to 1023
    show number Green ▼
```

Next, we are going to go back to the basic menu and drag a 'pause' command to underneath the 'show number green' command. Change the amount of seconds to 500ms (half a second). This will tell the system to pause for half a second before it shows the next number so that they don't all get muddled up together.

Next, copy the 'show number green' command and change the green to red using the arrow next to green. Put another 'pause' command underneath this.

CODING

```
on button A ▼ pressed
    set Green ▼ to pick random 0 to 1023
    set Red ▼ to pick random 0 to 1023
    set Blue ▼ to pick random 0 to 1023
    show number Green ▼
    pause (ms) 500 ▼
    show number Red ▼
    pause (ms) 500 ▼
```

Lastly, copy the 'show number red' command and change the red to blue. Put another pause underneath this. The whole finished code should look like this.

CODING

```
forever
    analog write pin P0 ▼ to Green ▼
    analog write pin P2 ▼ to Blue ▼
    analog write pin P1 ▼ to Red ▼
```

```
on button A ▼ pressed
    set Green ▼ to pick random 0 to 1023
    set Red ▼ to pick random 0 to 1023
    set Blue ▼ to pick random 0 to 1023
    show number Green ▼
    pause (ms) 500 ▼
    show number Red ▼
    pause (ms) 500 ▼
    show number Blue ▼
    pause (ms) 500 ▼
```

Download the code onto your Microbit. Press the A button and see what colour you get. Read the screen to find the 'colour code' of that colour.

Activity 22 – Making a flashing light

This project is going to make our LED light flash from one colour to another. We are going to be using the 'functions' menu which we haven't used before.

Start by going to makecode.microbit.org and starting a new project. Call this project something like 'flashing light'. You won't need the 'on start' command so you can get rid of this one but keep the 'forever' command which we will use later.

We are going to start by making a 'function'. A function is a group of commands. Click 'advanced' then click 'functions' then 'make a function'. This screen will appear.

Click where it says 'doSomething' and rename this function 'colour1'. Then click the green done button. This command will appear on your screen…

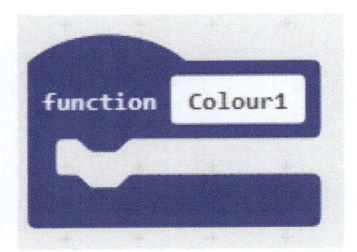

CODING

[function Colour1 block]

Inside this blue functions command we are going to be telling the system to send power to each of the three coloured lights.

Go to the 'pins' menu and drag an 'analogue write pin P0 to 1023' command into the 'function colour1' command block. Like this.

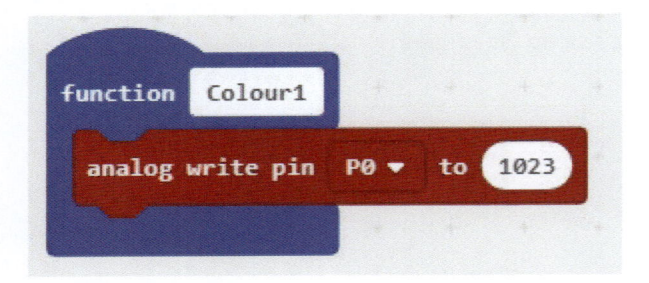

[function Colour1 with analog write pin P0 to 1023]

Next, grab two more 'analog write pin...' commands and put them underneath the first one. Change one to P1 and one to P2. Like this.

Page | 118

```
function Colour1
    analog write pin  P0 ▼  to  1023
    analog write pin  P1 ▼  to  1023
    analog write pin  P2 ▼  to  1023
```

At the moment, our function is sending full power to all three pins which would make white. You may want to leave this function as white or you may want to change it. I've changed mine to be full power to green and red and no power to blue. This will make the light appear yellow.

```
function Colour1
    analog write pin  P0 ▼  to  1023
    analog write pin  P1 ▼  to  1023
    analog write pin  P2 ▼  to  0
```

Let's make some more functions. You will have seen now that functions are just colours of light. The more functions we make,

Page | 119

the more different colours will be in our flashing light! If you want your light to just flash between two colours (e.g. blue and red like a police car) you just need to make two colours.

Make another function by going back to the functions menu and clicking 'make a function'. Call the next one 'colour2'. Inside the 'function colour2' command block that appears, copy three more 'analog write pin...' commands – one for each pin. Like this.

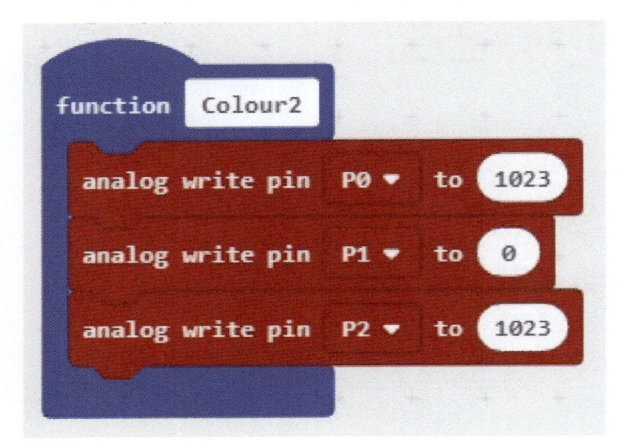

```
function Colour2
    analog write pin P0 ▼ to 1023
    analog write pin P1 ▼ to 0
    analog write pin P2 ▼ to 1023
```

You will notice, I've chosen to turn green and blue fully on and turn red fully off. This will make a cyan colour. You can choose whichever values you want, just make sure they are different enough from the values in 'function colour1' or else you won't notice your light changing colour if the two colours are too similar!

I've decided to make a light with three different colours so I'm going to make one more function and call it colour3. You may want to make lots more functions!

Here are all my functions together.

So, now that I have made all my functions, it's time to tell the system to flash between them. Now it's time to use the 'forever' command. You may need to zoom out if it's disappeared!

Go to your 'functions' menu and drag a 'call colour1' command into the 'forever' block. Like this.

Page | 121

CODING

This tells the system to change the light to the colour that we programmed inside 'colour1'. For my project, this is yellow.

Next, go back to the 'functions' menu and drag a 'call colour2' command under 'call colour1'.

```
forever
    call Colour1
    call Colour2
```

Keep going back to the 'functions' menu and getting the 'call colour...' commands until you have called all your functions. For me this looks like...

```
forever
    call Colour1
    call Colour2
    call Colour3
```

So, now we have told the system to flash between the three different lights. The problem at the moment is that it will flash through them much too fast and we won't be able to see the lights changing colour. We need to finish off by putting 'pause'

Page | 122

commands between the colours. Go to the 'basic' menu and drag a 'pause (ms) 200' command on to your screen. Put it between 'call colour1' and 'call colour2' and then change the amount of time by clicking the arrow next to the '200'. I've set mine at 500ms (half a second) which means the yellow light will stay on for half a second before changing to cyan.

```
forever
    call Colour1
    pause (ms) 500 ▼
    call Colour2
    call Colour3
```

Put a pause command after all your 'call colour...' commands. Like this.

CODING

```
forever
    call Colour1
    pause (ms) [500 ▼]
    call Colour2
    pause (ms) [500 ▼]
    call Colour3
    pause (ms) [500 ▼]
```

You are done! Download your code onto your Microbit and make sure your LED is connected properly. Your light should start flashing!

We hope you have enjoyed all these activities and have learned a lot along the way. Maybe you could even have a go at making your own Microbit projects or teaching a friend how to code.

For more Fun Science products including the additional components mentioned in this book, visit

www.fun-science.org.uk/shop

Page | 124

Printed in Great Britain
by Amazon